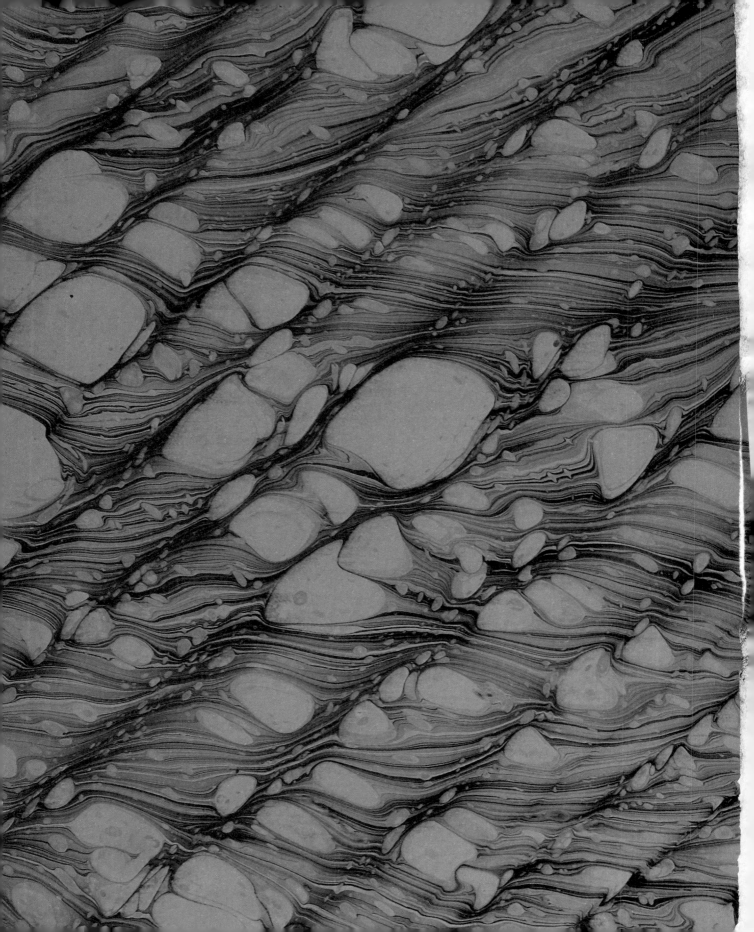

# OLD WORLD ITALIAN

### RECIPES & SECRETS
### *from our* TRAVELS IN ITALY

## MIMI THORISSON

*Photographs by Oddur Thorisson*

CLARKSON POTTER/
PUBLISHERS
*NEW YORK*

## TO MY FAMILY

CLARKSON POTTER is a trademark and POTTER
with colophon is a registered trademark of Penguin
Random House LLC.

Library of Congress Cataloging-in-Publication Data
is available upon request.

ISBN 978-1-9848-2359-5
eBook ISBN 978-1-9848-2360-1

Printed in China

Book and cover design by Stephanie Huntwork
Cover photographs by Oddur Thorisson

10 9 8 7 6 5 4 3 2 1

First Edition

# CONTENTS

# *INTRODUCTION*

FOR EIGHT YEARS I HAD BEEN LIVING, MOSTLY, IN FRENCH KITCHENS, amongst the copper pots and pans and the oily jars of duck fat stacked on swaying shelves betwixt the plum jams of early autumn, the cornichons, and the candied onions. I was happy in those kitchens: I had distanced myself from the city, and what a city it was. Who in their right mind would ever leave Paris? Later, I had no particular reason to leave my French country kitchen either—and a hundred good ones to stay. Yet Italy was calling us. After all, it was there where the seeds of our country life had been sown a decade earlier. All those holidays in Italy, by the sea in small, grand hotels with waiters in white jackets and Bellinis before dinner. In rented villas from Tuscany to Umbria to Marche. On road trips winding from north to south and on romantic holidays, including a honeymoon in Rome, Italy called us like a siren to a sailor, and we were powerless to refuse her. For a moment, or forever, we closed the shutters and doors to our magical palace at 1, rue de Loudenne in Médoc. We headed for a new adventure in this blessed, rich land, where the light is magical at any hour, where from north to south, east to west, fruits and vegetables grow with abandon, where the coffee is better and the paintings are older.

We came charging over the mountains in a car filled with children and dogs. We brought some pans, a few good knives, and a painting of a dog to place above our dining table. A dining table we had not yet found. We left almost everything in our house in France and brought very little. In a sense,

> *"Have you ever read music?" an old man in Rome once asked me.*
> *"It's very boring. You can't really read music, you must hear it. Food is the same: You must see it, smell it, eat it. A recipe is no good if nobody cooks from it."*

we were starting over, quite literally without even a pot to cook in. The first night of boiling pasta in Torino saw me running in a side street with a pot in hand, borrowed from a nearby seafood restaurant; and as if to keep to my French roots, I had a bottle of Champagne in the other. That was a beautiful evening; many have followed. There is magic in cooking, and in cooking Italian food there is alchemy. Every region has its dishes and every dish has its story. The story of a nation is a story of food. And now, in the most modest way, through this book, we are a part of that story.

## THE BOOK YOU HAVE IN YOUR HANDS IS, IN FACT, TWO BOOKS.

In part, it's my story, or rather, my family's: our Italy, how we have experienced her, the Italian food we have always cooked, always loved. These are the family classics inspired by our travels throughout the years and by the recipes and traditions I've fallen in love with during our first year living in Italy. It is also another book, one made possible by good people, Italians willing to share their best work, their family secrets, so I could then share them here with you. From regional treasures steeped in tradition to renegade versions of what Italian food can taste like when executed with flair, passion, and a touch of modernity, these are the "best of" recipes plucked from my Italian culinary dreams. Whether eating to live or living to eat, here, there is no difference, no pretension. Food is truly the fabric of life, the pleasure and passion. A humble necessity and the highest honor.

# *FROM BORDEAUX TO TORINO, SETTING THE STAGE*

### ENTERING THE LION'S DEN.

It was a conscious decision to leave it all behind and start our Italian lives with practically nothing. We preserved, fully intact, the house we had put so much love into, bringing hardly anything but our open minds and empty stomachs. Well, that was the theory anyway. My husband somehow expected all the kids to speak Italian after two weeks of private lessons, and when they didn't, he said it was "good for them." Sink or swim was the order of the day, and thankfully, they chose the latter, even if it wasn't all pretty.

We had talked about making an Italian cookbook together for years. It was always in the cards and in the stars. We felt we had traveled enough, that I had cooked enough, been in Italy often enough and long enough to mount a credible attempt. But in the end, we realized we needed to be here full time, as we have always lived our life rather than staged it. (The food I cook gets eaten, not just shot; the cutlery we use are our own knives and forks, not props. The rooms you see are where and how we live our lives.)

A holiday is when your habits are broken, when you do new things every day, try food for the first time. There is no routine, only adventure. But living in a place means adapting to a new routine, forming little habits that will take you a long way toward feeling like a local. On holiday, our conversation had always been, "Wouldn't it be nice if that great little coffee place were our hangout?" or "Wouldn't it be something if we could come here for lunch every day?" It was much the same thinking that had brought us out of Paris and deep into the countryside in southern France almost a decade earlier. Many good things start with "Wouldn't it be nice?" Then you do, and they are, and that's when things get scary—in the most exhilarating way.

We had spent so much time scouring Italy for the best food, the finest restaurants, for professional purposes but mostly for ourselves. I had cooked countless Italian meals, and we had been enamored of Italian food forever. Yet coming here was like entering the lions' den, climbing the wall where it is highest. It was a little frightening, but only the brave succeed.

## NOTHING IS POSSIBLE WITHOUT THE TABLE.

The apartment on Piazza Vittorio Veneto in Torino is beautiful: grand high ceilings with old inlaid parquet floors in most rooms and Venetian marble floors in others. A gorgeous fireplace in the living room, a spacious terrace overlooking the bustling square, perhaps the busiest in all of Torino. It was, however, greatly lacking in the *"bucolic sprezzatura"* that had become the signature of our rambling old country house north of Bordeaux. I remember waking up that first morning in an almost empty flat, no furniture save for a newly upholstered lounge chair in one corner and a reading light next to it. We had already found the most important furniture of any home: the kitchen and dining tables. For the kitchen, an oval marble design, a little fancy and bourgeois. The other, as humble and gorgeous as they come: a Piedmontese farm table, large enough to seat twelve people—our family and a guest or two. The dining chairs were a bargain, twenty of them, never used before, having waited a hundred years for us in a dusty cabinetmaker's reserve. They had holes where the seats were supposed to be, so we came up with a temporary solution, one of those temporary solutions that lasts forever.

That first morning in Torino, I was left to wonder if we had been too extreme in our "out of the comfort zone" approach. It's a strange sensation after years of presiding over not one but two dreamlike farmhouse kitchens and cooking feasts for up to thirty people at a time to then find yourself heating water for tea in a saucepan and having to borrow a pot from a nearby restaurant to boil your first pasta. Oddur had made sure we brought a corkscrew. (As he would.) But that was about it. He had said that having to buy everything again would make us feel young. That morning, it just made me feel frustrated.

Torino was closing down that week—bakers and butchers alike were headed for the seaside, restaurateurs were closing up shop without notifying the Internet. I am very particular about meat: where it comes from, the quality, and how the animals were treated. In Médoc, I had access to no fewer than five different butchers, each with their own specialty—one for poultry, one for veal, one just for his marvelous entrecôte, and so on. Eventually, I found a butcher in Torino that I liked. A very tanned one. But, of course, he shut down the next day, off to the beach to work on his tan.

Later on that first day, I took a walk on my own in the sweltering heat. I ventured up the columned sidewalk of via Po into piazza Castello where the positive powers of Torino reside. (The city is supposedly protected by the holy shroud of Turin and haunted by the devil himself.) Torino is a city of extremes, full of old families of prestige and power and new ones who came to work for Fiat in the 1950s and stayed even after the work had left. It's a majestic and mysterious town, full of Italians having coffee in the morning and drinks at night. A real city, not a city of tourists. And that's why we came here, and also why we'll stay.

Outside Caffè Torino in piazza San Carlo, there is a golden bull laid into the marbled terrace. His crotch has a little dent in it, and after a while you realize why. Locals passing by tap their toes into it, while the braver ones make a little pirouette, a full circle on one leg, which is not without risk. That morning, I attempted it for the first time. I had a cookbook to finish, a life to start, and I thought I might as well have the luck of the Taurus on my side. Especially as it's better to fall on marble than to fail in life.

July and August were the months of gelato. Each day, we had a new "best ice cream I ever had" moment—from *zabaione* to *farina bona* (corn) or a simple fior di latte. One place just opposite our apartment had the best Sicilian cassata flavor, which was later replaced by an equally delightful fig and ricotta version. The kids love *stracciatella* best. I'm fickle, so I still haven't decided. When everything else shut down, there was always gelato in the afternoon and *aperitivo* at 6 o'clock.

In those days of shuttered shops and restaurants, trips to the Ligurian coast or to the lakes of the Piemonte, walking in a half-closed city, having too many coffees, endless trips to the bookstore when we had no Internet (and regrettably fewer trips since), I had one valuable ally: the farmers' market in Porta Palazzo that never closed. It didn't even seem smaller than usual. Almost every morning, I headed there with a huge basket and would bring it back full. They say it's the best farmers' market in Europe, and they may be right. Under a cast-iron Belle Époque–style structure, a flock of farmers from Piemonte's agricultural areas gather every day but Sunday. They look the part, with rough hands and dirty boots, their stalls filled with bountiful produce, honest and delicious. Zucchini flowers that shine so brightly, and so many of them that they feel like an edible painting or rows of the calmest fireflies. (It's just a bright yellow color, of course, but I'm convinced they emit some kind of light—a yellow that bright is simply not possible without a beam from within.)

Sometimes I arrived in a hurry: It was late and I was hungry, or at least the kids were hungry. Other days, I stuck around, listened, observed. I weighed the difference between a French market and this market, between what I couldn't get here and what I could get in abundance there. In France, zucchini flowers are nigh impossible to come by, while here, just 100 kilometers to the southeast, they are everywhere. I observed, like a food detective, not only what people were buying, but also what they were to cook with it. Luckily, many Piedmontese speak good French, which made the culinary conversation a lot easier. Everyone was happy to share their secrets with me. Or at least some of their secrets.

In the middle of a hot summer, it was the produce that excited me most, the bottomless pit of vegetables I had until now considered rare or hard to get. What's more, the guanciale we used to hunt for in France or bring back from Italy, and then savor like a treasure, was now everywhere and for every day. Later, in the fall, puntarelle, my husband's favorite, was no longer something you'd have to order in advance from a special purveyor, but rather a garden variety vegetable, a dime a dozen.

### EVERY GOOD STORY—AND I HOPE THIS IS ONE OF THOSE—HAS A MOMENT WHERE EVERYTHING SEEMS LOST.

Mine came sometime in August, when in good spirits, with a glass of something delicious in hand, I attempted to cook my first very serious meal in my kitchen in Torino. I had managed many lovely meals there already, but this time I went a bit further, channeling my enormous kitchen in France, where grilling over grapevines in the fireplace and overseeing ten pots of deliciousness at once was everyday business. I was cooking some meat . . . memory escapes me what. I got carried away and went into full-on flambé mode. Not a good idea. The stove hood took fire and the whole kitchen burst into flame. My mother-in-law, Johanna, was next to me and witnessed the whole thing. Both of us were stunned. What in Médoc would have been an everyday exercise was impossible here. The kitchen was saved. More or less. But my spirit was hurt, my cooking mojo deflated.

"It's never about the equipment," my husband, the photographer, always says. When a lens on his Canon breaks, he just uses another. If that breaks as well, he'll reach for his phone. Use what you have. Limitations are a blessing in disguise—it has a nice ring to it, but does it actually work? Cooking, like taking photos, is more about ingredients and technique than appliance. A state-of-the-art stove, a slick, expensive camera—those are some of life's pleasures. But do they really contribute to the art of cooking or the art of making pictures? I was finding that out all summer in my own way. Would I rather cook on my trusted Lacanche? Yes, I love her and miss her. Can I still cook well without her? Also yes. Absolutely yes.

It was a long, hot summer of some victories and delights, and some disgruntlements, too, but mainly just prolonged and sweaty family time in an empty and hot and elegant apartment. Every day was pretty much about "What's for lunch?" and "What's for dinner?," which wasn't much of a departure from our French country life or our Parisian life before that. In the end, after all that, when I was neither winning nor losing in my battle with this book, I had a breakthrough.

In late August, the stores had started to open again. From under sliding metal doors they revealed themselves: the curious retailers and establishments that had been hidden all summer. The streets suddenly seemed longer than they had before as they had more to offer, and walking down them went more slowly due to all the new distractions that hadn't been there days before.

I woke up early one day and heard the older children already fighting over focaccia in the kitchen. Instead of joining the battle, I escaped quietly and ran down the stairs, turned left when I entered piazza Vittorio, and headed swiftly down via della Rocca, or as we call it, "our street." (Quite a gentrified street, but really one with everything that a couple like us could need or want.) I walked past the incredibly well-dressed gentlemen who would every day outdress the devil in a store named "Lucifer Is an Honest Man," then past the posh little corner store where we send our daughter Louise to get ham every night (and they love her for it). Past two of our favorite restaurants (what luck that is—the luck of the devil?), past the little square with a garden where we had *aperitivo* almost every night in August, a place of such routine that you can tell the time just by looking at the clientele. (Around 4 or 5 o'clock in the afternoon, it's full of kids up to age eighteen, smoking and drinking coffee, many stylishly dressed and nobody touching any alcohol. After that, it's the slightly more grown-up crowd;

everyone has a drink of bright red or orange and a huge plate of what should really be called dinner, but is disguised as something else.) Past the women's shoe store with beautiful Argentinian shoes where I bought a pair in July that I have never worn. I walked past the beautiful door at No. 29 and past the incredibly expensive antiques and textiles store where we once almost bought a table but didn't because we weren't insane. Past the other stylish menswear shop where I always admire the tailoring in the window and wish for a very brief moment that I were a man (the store has now been replaced by a flower store).

Finally, I arrived at via Mazzini, the street of butchers, grocers, little restaurants, and a miscellany of other things. One place, very plain looking, had a woman in the window making pasta. She seemed very, very good at it, so I stuck around and after a good while, I became self-conscious, feeling a little weird just staring at her through the glass. Eventually, I ventured inside of what is a little store that sells fresh pasta and a few other items. They have four tables where you can sit, so I went back later that day with my family. Soon the kids were taking pasta classes every Friday and I always tagged along. These may have been the most significant, meaningful moments of my time in Torino up to that point. After months of not being quite sure, sometimes doubting myself, even when I was enjoying my life, I finally understood. Here, little girls and boys (but mainly girls) made pasta in such an effortless and unpretentious way. Mainly, they came with their mothers. Some were part of the family who owns the place. It was natural for them, normal. And for me, it was eye-opening. I saw my own daughters making such progress, graduating rapidly from "Sweetheart, that's so great" to "Wow, that's actually great." I finally felt at home, felt I belonged. It's a family thing, a place where children cook with their parents, where making food from scratch, and great food at that, is ordinary, and where the idea is not just to buy but to make. That's the kind of place where I belong.

Eventually, I enrolled myself for more advanced lessons. Whole afternoons of nothing but kneading, sculpting, cutting, and filling various raviolis, creating different pasta shapes, strands, and strings. I have been fortunate enough to cook alongside and observe some great Italian cooks, both home cooks and celebrated chefs. I have made a career out of going to restaurants, cooking in my own kitchen, inspiring myself, and getting inspired by others. And yet that first afternoon with Claudia opened a door to a new dimension for me. Not because I hadn't made pasta before, but because somehow I was now one of them. The pasta-making ladies in the paintings. The hard-working women who go about their business with staunch professionalism, pride, and knowledge. Some people do yoga, while some have a life coach, a shrink, or a personal trainer. A golf pro may need a swing doctor to get his game back on track. I have Claudia, my pasta coach, and she made me feel like I had finally arrived in Torino. Two months after I had.

## I am French. Or rather, half-French, if you can be such a thing. I am not Italian.

They are two great kitchens, the Italian and the French. French cooking is in my blood; it's in my nature to cook with butter and duck fat. To start the day with a flaky croissant and to finish it with cheese and wine. French cooking, while mysterious and complicated to some, is strangely democratic. It's centralized cooking: All the good stuff, sooner or later, came to Paris, and what the Parisians liked, everybody liked. The French kitchen is accessible and overwhelming at the same time. It's a canon rather than a curiosity. Open to everyone, though not everyone dares.

Italian cooking has a reputation for being simpler, easier, more ingredient-based. That is, of course, not even half the truth. It's also known, rightly so, to be much more regional and varied. What you eat in Napoli is nothing like the food of Milano. Some good dishes and ideas have spread throughout the country, but Italian cooking, especially home cooking, remains largely regional.

When we drive from Bordeaux to Torino, we like to think of it as a journey of two colors. From the regal blue of France to the warmer yellow of Italy. Coming out of the Fréjus Road Tunnel, heading down the valley that takes us to Torino, there is a change in the light. Italy is a warmer country. The people are warm—fierce, too, but warm nonetheless. Italians like seeing big families, mothers with children. They are happy to see kids in restaurants. And dogs, too. Manners are important, but not as important as in France. The police are nicer; people run red lights without hesitation (which I do not recommend, but it's a telling sign).

# REGIONAL ITALIAN COOKING

I have often toyed with the idea that all the dishes of Italian cuisine are tantamount to the entire musical repertoire of a famous band or a singer, someone who's been around forever and is still going strong. The dishes everyone knows, the universally beloved ones, are the ultimate "Best of Collection." These are the recipes people have cooked at home, names they expect and demand to see on the menus of "Italian restaurants." They are the international ambassadors of Italian cuisine—fried calamari, minestrone, spaghetti alla carbonara, penne all'arrabbiata, veal Milanese, tiramisù, panna cotta. Dishes cooked all over Italy and all over the world.

Some have their origins attached to the title, like Risotto alla Milanese or Ragù Bolognese, but otherwise, they're just Italian. It's common knowledge, I guess, that pizza comes from Naples, that tomatoes are prevalent in the south, and there's a vague idea that northern cuisine is heavier on meat. Others may know that dried pasta is traditionally used more in the south while the fresh egg version is stronger in the north. Restaurant menus are reshuffled and refocused, dishes reimagined or reinvented, but in the end, it's just a new release of all our favorite songs. And for the most part, we have no complaints.

Italy has twenty regions, each with its own distinctive cuisine, developed in tandem with nature and influenced by its neighbors. These regional styles are the LPs, the individual albums. The most popular ones have quite a few songs on the "Best of" album—regions like Lazio (Rome), Lombardia (Milano), and Campania (Napoli) have no complaints. Some of the lesser known regions are lucky to get one song into the repertoire. People who like Italian food know the "Best ofs." People who really *love* Italian food are quite familiar with most of the regional "albums" but might not remember exactly where this or that dish came from, on which album it was featured. Then you have the nerds, buffs, and connoisseurs who not only know the dishes of each region, but also the B-sides, the outtakes, the dishes nobody serves in restaurants and can only be had in somebody's home, probably cooked by his or her grandmother. It's all Italian cooking, but the biggest hits are not always the best songs.

When I was cooking the recipes for this book, I often found myself needing some tool or other to do it properly (remember that we left basically everything in France; even a cheese grater feels exotic when you don't have one). I found a small store near our house, a proper kitchen shop, very neat, no frills, professional, historic—and with all the tools I could possibly ever need. The owners are a father and son, very knowledgeable, helpful, and interested. You have to ring a bell to gain entrance, and when you do, you hear their grumpy little dog in the back room, telling you he's guarding the premises (sort of). It became a ritual. I would enter, and the son, in the front room, would ask, "What are you making today?" As I told him, I would know that his father was in the back room, door half shut, listening, maybe because he still thinks, after all these years, that there might come a moment when his son gives the wrong advice and he'll need to step in. Often, I would say that I was cooking this dish from that town in a certain region. Almost every time, the father would come out, shaking his head, saying only, "No, no, no. You can't say that. It doesn't come from there; it comes from somewhere else" or "Nobody knows" or "It comes from all the north." It's a compliment for a dish, I guess, when everybody claims it.

We have always liked and practiced the idea of eating locally and seasonally, and while the notion has gained popularity in recent times, it seems that Italians have always eaten this way. Aided, of course, by their division (Italy wasn't united as one country until 1861), each region stuck to its guns and cooked its own recipes with homegrown produce. Rival towns weren't keen on swapping recipes or sharing new varieties of vegetables with their foes. The prosperous and meat-rich north took inspiration from neighbors like France and Austria, while Arab and Spanish influences are evident in the south. The way we have discovered Italy, over a long period of time, one region at a time, allows for an enhanced appreciation of what each region is all about and why. We would probably never drink Lambrusco outside of Emilia-Romagna (because for the most part, we don't like it enough) or have a carbonara in a restaurant anywhere else but Rome (because it's too good there to have it anywhere else).

Local is the opposite of Global, yet the two can, on a good day, find synergy. It's wonderful to share information, discover, and mix and mingle. To be able to cook an obscure, unknown dish from a little known region in your home kitchen, preferably, or at least partially, with locally grown produce. To have access to the ingredients and techniques from a far-flung locale is a privilege other generations did not experience. Sourcing information online is easy, and access to produce is improving everywhere. But you need to know what to look for; someone has to push you in the right direction, and Global doesn't always do that. Sometimes he rears his ugly head and takes over, streamlines, eliminates. Only the "Best of" survives, the accessible and easy to sell. When Global plays ball with Local, he's a swell guy. When he goes it alone, he sometimes destroys and takes down traditions.

## LIFE, LOVE, FOOD. IT'S ALL ABOUT BALANCE. LIKE LOCAL AND GLOBAL.

In writing this book, I focused on the regions I know best, like best, wanted to know more about. I visited them all again, trying hard to notice the differences and similarities. I closed my eyes and opened my mouth. I listened to people. I was thirsty for more knowledge and I was hoping for inspiration. I was not disappointed.

The cuisine of each of the twenty regions of Italy deserves its own book. At least. History is important, and so is geography, but we won't go into that too much. My wish is that the reader enjoy the reading, but especially the food, the recipes. That's what this book is about. But as I like to say, a recipe always tastes better when it comes with a good story. Throughout the book, you'll find essays on the various regions we cover—I don't think of them as definitive accounts, but rather as my portraits of places, how I see them, how they affect me. What their food means to me.

I have gained much knowledge on Italian cooking in the past few years and not least since I started working on this book. Yet, I am not Italian.

Sometimes that's a good thing, adding a fresh point of view. On the other hand, I wanted insider access, authenticity, the perspective and knowledge of those who have always lived here. Most regions in this book are represented by one or more people who cherish food as I do, who have a passion for cooking and a love for their region that they are happy to share. These are my good Italians who opened their arms and their doors. As I revisit the regions through my writing, looking at Oddur's photos, and remembering our time together, they seem to me like characters in a play and it all feels a little unreal. Was I really there, with all those people—or was it all a movie?

# *EATING ITALIAN*

Selecting the recipes for this book was one of the most fun headaches I've ever had. Eventually, I cut them down, but I could easily have selected completely different ones that would have been just as good, as representative, as special as the ones I chose. It is a good headache to have and speaks volumes of the vastness of material available to anyone who dives into Italian cooking. I have some experience: two French cookbooks to my name. Those books taught me a lot about the process, but also about the reactions of readers, what they want, and how their "wants" vary. Also what I want, which is to write a book that's useful, that I would like to have in my own kitchen. A book that I'm proud of and that does justice to the subject of Italian food.

Italian cooking is one of the most recognizable and celebrated styles in the world. But only parts of it. One of the touchstones in my head was that the book must include a good number of dishes that people already know, from restaurants or from home. Very good versions of these classic dishes that are accessible and achieve the best results in the easiest way—but without compromise. I also wanted to introduce new dishes, recipes readers might never have heard of or, if they have, never tried themselves. I wanted to include my personal favorites, my own family cooking, the recipes that have followed me for years. I wanted the selection to be eclectic, unscientific, whimsical, and partially down to chance. Like how I decide to cook every day. It's never a question of "We had fish two days in a row so we should have meat today"—it's about what I want to eat on that day, and this book is a reflection of that, hopefully not unbalanced, but personal and real. I believe that most of the recipes in this book are easy or fairly easy to make, and the ingredients are not too far-fetched. I also wanted to give you a few to dream about, for when you're ready to invest the time and take the leap.

Italian food is known to be very ingredient-based, not surprising since Italy has always had some of the best ingredients in the world. The dictum being that while the French treat produce with the approach of "now what can we do to this food to make it complicated and elevated," the Italians are more prone to let the ingredients shine, meaning many dishes have four ingredients or fewer, and sometimes olive oil and salt are all you need. As I said before, this is, of course, an oversimplification; there are overlaps between the two cuisines as well. But in general, this adage is somewhat true. Accessibility is another element to consider. The world fell in love with Italian food a long time ago. Italian food is everywhere. Pizza is the ultimate takeout. Pasta with store-bought sauce is a quick fix when there is no time to waste. But what is accessible becomes ordinary. We love it, but take it for granted. French cooking has long been reserved for chefs with intimidating moustaches or the mythical *mères* of Lyon who cook legendary dishes nobody in their right mind would attempt at home. (Admittedly, this is not exactly true: French cooking can be perfectly accessible, but the legend is there and puts French food on a pedestal that it might not even want to be on.)

I've been thinking about tortellini. People have it all the time; it's considered everyday food. Decent versions are available in most supermarkets—put some sauce on it and voilà, dinner is served. People generally don't consider the dish as festive or sophisticated, but that's how all the raviolis started out: for celebrations, special occasions. The rich meat filling itself was a luxury. The hours of rolling, by hand, individual raviolis, maybe for a hundred people, was painstaking. Homemade tortellini, or freshly made at the local *pastificcio*, is in no way comparable to the supermarket variety that lasts a month in your fridge. A good *tortellini in brodo* is exalted cuisine, fit for a king. In Italy, it's common to serve the tortellini in festive context, during Christmas and New Year's. Other cultures might find this strange, as it's the food they have when there is no time, or what they have in simple trattorias when on holiday in Italy or somewhere else. The lines are blurred as it's not just what you eat, but how well it is made. There is spaghetti with tomato sauce and there is spaghetti with tomato sauce—and the latter can be a culinary masterpiece.

Cooking has always been about creating good food—sure, with various degrees of refinement, for different people and occasions, but that's been the main objective. Nowadays, a talented chef who wants to be noticed or celebrated needs to do more than just cook good food. He needs to be creative, inventive; his food needs to be new. New is good when it leads to improvements. It's a positive thing when we ask questions of the food we eat: how it can be tastier, healthier, friendlier to the planet. New for the sake of new, however, is not very interesting to me. The final verdict on how good something is must always be rendered by the mouth. It can be fascinating to hear about some clever, new way to use an ingredient. But it needs to be better or at least as good as the old way of using the ingredient. Which is why I am very appreciative of the chefs I admire, who are skilled enough to cook anything, creative enough to dazzle you with their process and technique, yet devote at least some of their energy to the much less egocentric work of making the best version of something that already exists. The best carbonara, a truly great roast chicken. There is something very beautiful, respectful, and ultimately delicious in looking for the new inside the old.

I used to find the idea of eating a full Italian menu hard to swallow. Literally. The idea of starting with cured meats, olives, crostini, assorted vegetables. Moving on to pasta and then having to face a pork roast, a bird, a steak, never mind the cheese, and finally dessert. I found it daunting. Exhilarating, but daunting. It was the pasta that got me, the rest I could handle. I was always more of a pasta or meat kind of girl, rarely both. This caused some controversy in the family. My husband loves restaurants. *Loves.* He can sit for hours, linger, the longer the service takes, the better. He has incredible tolerance for wine. I'm a little bit more impatient and a cheaper date when it comes to alcohol. He would order the full menu; I would either risk getting bored or follow suit, which was fun, but heavy. Once, in Torino, we went for lunch in a very traditional restaurant. I had bought a beautiful vintage dress that morning and was impatiently and proudly wearing it. Green, lacy, a little bit sexy, tight in the right places, very early '60s Sophia Loren. Toward the end of the meal, very full and probably tipsy, too, I had to sneeze and the dress split completely open on one side. Oddur lent me his jacket, the least he could do, but it made me think: How can one navigate a meal like that without ending up naked? The answer was easy to find. Portions. The whole traditional Italian menu of antipasti, *primi, secondi,* and more is based on family meals; and at home you don't order from a menu nor does everyone have a dish of their own. A bowl of pasta on the table is for all to share, so is the meat that follows. Portions in restaurants are not tailored for meals like this; it's rare to see people order the full five courses, unless they share. At home, everybody has the same thing, and that suits the Italian menu perfectly. In restaurants, we've come up with a formula: A few antipasti for the table. Then everybody has their own pasta or rice. (I give some of mine to the youngest.) Then one or two meat dishes to share. Dessert is optional, in theory, but we always have it.

# (UNLOCKING) THE SECRETS TO ITALIAN COOKING

## THREE BASIC STOCKS

When people ask me for cooking advice, one of the first things I usually suggest is making their own stock or broth. Lots of it. All the time. Stock is often misunderstood and seems to scare people away. I have friends who look through cookbooks in search of a recipe they think they can muster, and when the recipe includes making stock, they flip to the next one. Stock, once made every day or every week in most households, has become a frightening thought to many, especially younger people who have grown up without that pot constantly simmering on the kitchen stove. Stock, they think, is what chefs make in stainless-steel kitchens with industrial-size pots. In reality, stock is the easiest recipe you will ever make. It's also quite forgiving: It will improve any recipe, and while it can be extremely delicious when done well, it's rarely bad. How difficult is it to throw some meat and vegetables, or just vegetables, into a pot with water and bring it to a boil? Let it simmer while you cook other things or watch a movie or read a book. It's also the perfect way to make use of vegetables that are on their way out.

The stock can be stored in the fridge for a couple of days or frozen for much longer, and if you have that stock waiting, you are empowered, your possibilities almost infinite. You can make a last-minute risotto. A vegetable soup. A delicious sauce. If you are not a regular stock maker, I suggest, before I suggest anything else, that you become one; stock making involves very little effort and offers the richest reward. Here are three of my staple stocks that I absolutely make all the time. Only the oxtail stock requires a little procuring; the ingredients for the others you probably have in your home already.

# Oxtail Stock
*Makes about 3 quarts / liters*

I call this stock the elixir of my life. It's particularly special because not only is it incredibly tasty, but it is also, on a personal level, very important to my health. It is extremely nourishing and I make it once a week, having a cup every morning in winter and spring for extra nourishment and comfort. My family always said that this was the secret to longevity, beauty, and good bones, so I can't live without it!

6 TO 7 POUNDS / 3 KG OXTAIL (4 TO 5 PIECES), TRIMMED OF EXCESS FAT

2 TABLESPOONS EXTRA-VIRGIN OLIVE OIL

2 ONIONS, UNPEELED AND HALVED

2 CARROTS, COARSELY CHOPPED

4 CELERY STALKS, COARSELY CHOPPED

2 BAY LEAVES

1 TEASPOON BLACK PEPPERCORNS

A HANDFUL OF PARSLEY STEMS

⅔ CUP / 160 ML DRY WHITE WINE OR SHERRY

2 TABLESPOONS FINE SEA SALT

1  Preheat the oven to 440°F / 220°C.

2  Place the oxtail on a large baking sheet and drizzle with the olive oil. Roast until sizzling and browned, 20 to 25 minutes.

3  Place the browned meat and the onions, carrots, and celery in a large stockpot (at least 6 quarts / liters). Add the bay leaves, peppercorns, and parsley stems. Fill the pot with enough cold water to cover by 1 to 2 inches / 2.5 to 5 cm. Add the wine and bring to a boil over medium-high heat. Skim excess scum and reduce the heat to low. Stir in the salt. Cover with a lid and cook for 3 to 6 hours (the longer the better). Pass the stock through a sieve, reserving the oxtail meat for another use.

4  Let cool before refrigerating for up to 3 days or storing in the freezer for up to 4 months. (Once cooled, the stock will set into a thick brown jelly.)

NOTE: *To make a bouquet garni, combine 5 sprigs of thyme, 1 sprig each of sage, rosemary, oregano, and parsley, and 1 bay leaf in a small bunch and tie together with kitchen twine.*

# Chicken Stock
*Makes about 6 cups / 1.5 liters*

2 TABLESPOONS EXTRA-VIRGIN OLIVE OIL

2 POUNDS / 900 G CHICKEN CARCASS,
CUT INTO 4 PIECES

2 CARROTS, COARSELY CHOPPED

1 SHALLOT, SLICED

1 LEEK, SLICED

1 CELERY STALK, SLICED INTO CHUNKS

1 GARLIC CLOVE, SMASHED AND PEELED

1 TEASPOON BLACK PEPPERCORNS

1 BOUQUET GARNI (SEE NOTE OPPOSITE)

½ CUP / 120 ML DRY WHITE WINE

1 TABLESPOON FINE SEA SALT

1 LARGE YELLOW ONION, PEELED AND HALVED,
WITH 2 WHOLE CLOVES STUCK INTO EACH HALF

1   In a large stockpot, heat the olive oil over medium heat. Add the chicken carcass, carrots, shallot, leek, celery, garlic, peppercorns, and bouquet garni. Toss until the chicken is browned on all sides.

2   Add the white wine and cook for 2 minutes to reduce. Add 2 quarts / liters water, the salt, and onion. Bring to a boil and reduce the heat to low. Continue to simmer for 3 hours, uncovered. Strain the stock through a sieve.

3   Let cool before refrigerating for up to 3 days or store in the freezer for up to 4 months.

# Vegetable Stock
*Makes about 6 cups / 1.5 liters*

2 ONIONS, PEELED AND HALVED

3 CARROTS, COARSELY CHOPPED

4 CELERY STALKS, COARSELY CHOPPED

4 SPRIGS OF FRESH THYME

1 BAY LEAF

2 SPRIGS OF FRESH PARSLEY

1 TEASPOON BLACK PEPPERCORNS

1   In a large stockpot, combine all the ingredients plus 2 quarts / liters water. (Less water means that your stock will be more concentrated; more water makes a lighter flavored stock.) Bring to a boil over medium-high heat. Reduce the heat to low and continue to simmer for 3 hours. Halfway through, stir all the vegetables.

2   Strain the stock through a sieve. Let cool before refrigerating for up to 3 days or storing in the freezer for up to 3 months.

# *APERITIVI & ANTIPASTI*

The two guilty pleasures of Italian eating both start with the letter A. Sometimes there is no clear distinction between them, especially nowadays. *Aperitivo* is both the moment when you have your pre-dinner drink and the drink itself. It just means work is over, fun and food will be had. And some of that food will be had now. All the usual suspects: olives, mini pizzas, deep-fried delicacies, some veggies thrown in for good measure. Basically, all the food that your personal trainer—if you're unlucky, or disciplined, enough to have one—will tell you not to eat. *Aperitivo* in its purest form is a vertical affair, standing up, because you still can. There is no written rule about standing, but that's the traditional way, at the bar, although many people, understandably, prefer sitting down for this part of the evening. Then there is antipasti, the other A: You're in the restaurant or at home, and by now you are surely sitting down. Curious concoctions have given way to wine. That's an absolute. The food quality usually goes up—no cheap, deep-fried thrills, and if there are, they're top-notch. This is the hour of really good hams, carefully prepared vegetables, quality crostini, cold salads, mixed seafood perhaps. You go for sparkling or you go straight to still. I have long thought that the most elegant thing anyone can have at this moment of the meal is the finest culatello and a very good glass of sparkling wine. Go for all the other stuff at your own peril and your own pleasure.

# BICERIN

*Espresso with Chocolate and Whipped Cream*

*Serves 4*

2 CUPS / 500 ML
WHOLE MILK

6 OUNCES / 180 G
UNSWEETENED
DARK CHOCOLATE,
CHOPPED INTO
SMALL PIECES

4 DOUBLE-SHOT
ESPRESSOS
(50 ML EACH),
THE STRONGER
THE BETTER

½ CUP / 120 ML
HEAVY CREAM,
WHIPPED

COFFEE BEANS
(OPTIONAL)
FOR GARNISH

This is nothing less than the official drink of Torino—no other drink has such a special place in the hearts of the city's inhabitants. Every café has its own version, which is very much a variation on the same theme, though the standard varies greatly. To me, the success lies in the quality of the ingredients (as always) and the care in preparation. *Bicerin* means "a small glass" in Piedmontese dialect, and that glass should be transparent so you can see all the layers (they shouldn't mix). The drink dates back to the eighteenth century, when espresso hadn't yet been invented; the coffee was different then, and the cream was not whipped but foamed. Today, many cafés serve a whipped cream version, and since I adore whipped cream, that's the version we'll use. I guess my love for whipped cream trumps my traditional side.

1  In a medium saucepan, heat the milk over low heat. When it starts to simmer slightly, add the chocolate pieces and whisk until melted and the mixture starts to boil. Continue whisking until foamy, about 2 minutes.

2  Fill the bottom third of four clear, heatproof glasses with the warm chocolate mixture. Pour an espresso into each over the back of a spoon. Finish with a layer of whipped cream. Top with coffee beans, if desired. Let the drink settle for a minute before serving.

# CAFFÈ SHAKERATO

*Serves 1*

6 ICE CUBES

1 DOUBLE-SHOT
ESPRESSO (50 ML),
PREFERABLY A
ROBUST BLEND

2 TEASPOONS /
10 ML SIMPLE SYRUP
(OPTIONAL)

3 COFFEE BEANS
(OPTIONAL)

Torino is the city of *aperitivo*. It seems like every evening at around 6 o'clock, the whole town gathers for a drink and something to eat, whether salty or crunchy or cheesy. I love to do it, too, but I can't do it every day, so shakerato is my salvation. You meet friends in a café or bar and they'll have a Negroni or a spritz and sometimes I'll join in, but other days, I'll order my trusted shakerato, which is shaken coffee with ice. It's served with the same ceremony as a Bellini, in a high glass, delightfully foamy, topped with three coffee beans. It's having a drink without having one, all the glamour and effect without the alcohol and calories.

1 Put the ice into a cocktail shaker. Add the espresso and syrup (if using) and shake hard until the shaker is frosted and the mixture has developed a sort of espresso foam, about 20 seconds.

2 Strain into a chilled cocktail glass and top with the coffee beans, if desired. Serve immediately.

# NOTES ON ITALIAN COFFEE
*Oddur Thorisson*

WHEN MY WIFE WAS WRITING HER SECOND cookbook, *French Country Cooking*, she asked me to write a few thoughts on French wine. In that essay, I mentioned my love for both coffee and wine, confessing I knew very little about coffee, except that the best coffee was to be found in Italy. This time, since I've devoted an unhealthy amount of time to coffee in the years since, she asked me to write about coffee.

I still think that the best coffee in the world is found in Italy. That's fact number one. And mind you, when I say fact, I just mean my opinion. Espresso was invented in Italy—that's an actual fact—so all coffee bars are essentially serving an Italian invention. Italian coffee is not about the actual coffee beans—it is a technique, or series of techniques. (In fact, no coffee is grown in Italy. Most of their beans come from places like Brazil, India, Vietnam, Colombia, Ghana, Ethiopia, or Jamaica, where the conditions and climate are ideal.) Other countries have mastered the Italian technique of espresso, but nowhere in the world is coffee as consistently good as it is here. Australians have somehow developed a real love for Italian coffee and are very good at making it. So are the Scandinavians, who drink more coffee than anyone. Nowadays, you can find good coffee everywhere, even in France, the stronghold of bad coffee. But it's not necessarily the norm. For every barista-style coffee bar in Paris, with carefully roasted beans and thoughtful preparation, you have countless other institutions that simply press a button and couldn't care less what splurts into your cup.

Italians generally like their coffee more roasted, even burnt, than a lot of modern, hipster baristas, who usually prefer a 100 percent arabica—more finely roasted, more acidic, and fruitier. Neither style is better than the other, but I prefer the Italian style. (So do the Italians.) Almost all coffee beans are either arabica or robusta. Robusta is more bitter and higher in caffeine; it's easier to grow and has traditionally been cheaper. Thus, it has gained a reputation for being of lesser quality, especially outside Italy. This is not true; you can have good or bad versions of both arabica and robusta. A lot of leading coffee brands very visibly put "100% Arabica" on their products, as if it means higher quality; like free-range chicken versus caged. But it's far from the truth. Though traditionally much of the arabica was of a higher quality than the robusta on the market, it's not about which bean, but about how well the coffee is made. Our friends the Vergnanos, owners of Caffè Vergnano, the oldest coffee roasting company in Italy, have some of the best coffee in the world, and their style suits my taste. Though (as I mentioned) a lot of coffee companies prefer arabica (including Illy), many others, like Vergnano, use a blend of both, typically 10 to 15 percent robusta and the rest arabica. In the south, the ratio of robusta is often higher, even much higher.

In Italy, you don't ask for espresso. You ask for *un caffè*, which means espresso. If you ask for

espresso, you are obviously not Italian. In my case, however, they still respond to my *"un caffè"* with "espresso or American coffee?" because I'm obviously not Italian to them, which is disheartening, but not enough to deter me. And all Italian coffee begins with espresso. Then they add milk: A cappuccino is a double espresso with a lot of steamed milk; a macchiato, my favorite, much less milk. But you probably knew that.

To me, the most important thing about a perfect espresso is the dark, thick cream, the all-important *crema*, that little seal of foam at the top of your cup. It needs to be creamy and thick; an espresso that doesn't have this has no reason to live. It's like a flat Champagne, the flavor might be incredible, yet . . . (It's easier to make a good *crema* with robusta, which is one of the reasons to include it in a blend.)

A delightful thing everywhere in Italy is that you can still get a great cup of coffee for one euro or one euro twenty. That is, if you have it at the counter. But why would you want to be anywhere else? The bar is often very beautiful, the barman nice and chatty. It's customary to stand next to other people also having their shot of espresso or cappuccino in the morning. Which reminds me, it's sort of a faux pas to have a cappuccino after lunch, but only sort of. Of course you can do what you want, but the majority of Italians have only a shot of espresso after lunch, which makes perfect sense if you think about it. Another faux pas, if there are any really, is drinking that cute little glass of fizzy water they serve with your cup after the coffee. It's meant to hydrate, clean your palate. If you need to clean your palate after the coffee, well, it's not exactly a great review.

The most important ingredient in any cup of coffee is time. Care and time. Of course it's better to have a good product to start with. And a decent machine. But how often have you walked into a café where they have coffee from a respectable roaster and a fancy Italian machine, and the coffee is awful? And it costs five euros. You don't need to drink or smell the coffee to get a good idea of what it will taste like. You can see it: You order a coffee, the lackluster barman nonchalantly grinds it and tamps it, rams it into the machine, and presses a button. The cup is full in 5 seconds. You might as well pour it into the sink—a 5-second coffee can never, ever be good. Maybe they just want to be quick. Maybe the customers don't care. Maybe you're in Paris. (By the way, I have nothing against Paris. I love Paris; everything is wonderful about Paris. Except the coffee.)

You notice I said, "The cup is full in 5 seconds." That's another thing: The cup should never be full, far from it. A long espresso is an aberration, an illusion that doesn't exist. An espresso, by definition, is 25 ml and should leave space for a lot of milk if desired. You can of course have a double, but that just means two espressos in the same cup.

Let's say you find a really good bread store and you ask the baker for his secret. Chances are, what makes the biggest difference is how long he lets the dough rise. If someone gives you an incredible glass of wine, chances are the year on the label is from a time your hair wasn't gray and you didn't need glasses to write your thoughts about coffee. I once met a pasta maker in Abruzzo. The best one. What's the difference between his pasta and the one you buy at the supermarket? I asked, genuinely curious as dried pasta basically has two ingredients and one of them is water. Theirs, he said, takes 2 hours to make; his is made in 48 hours. Time. One day, I'll write a book about the subject that will expose my contradictions. I'm prone to shortcuts, like in writing this piece (I bet you knew that, too), but I understand the value of time. It's food for thought.

To sum it up: If I were given the choice of a mediocre barman with great coffee beans or a great barman with mediocre coffee beans, I would choose the latter, every time. Screwing up good coffee beans is the easiest thing, but a good barista can make a decent cup from, well . . . not exactly anything, but anything within reason.

Finally, a thought on take-out coffee. That's really the darnedest invention. And no, I'm not being patronizing here; I, too, saw some glamour in the paper cup once upon a time. You know, when my hair was darker and all that. No coffee ever tasted better in paper than porcelain. That's not just a fact, but a truth. Nobody ever had a better conversation at his desk, sipping his coffee while on social media, than standing next to another actual person at the bar, taking in the scene around him. It's not about having enough time. Coffee doesn't take long to drink; it should be drunk immediately.

Here in Torino, if you order coffee and they notice you are too busy chatting or you have to take a phone call or if your kid throws a fit or your spouse throws a fit or your dog runs out into the piazza and you have to chase it, they immediately pour out the old one and give you a new, free one when you are ready. That's knowing your business. Of course, if it's the spouse who throws the fit, they'll probably also pour you a Negroni. That's really knowing your business.

# NENCIA CORSINI'S BLOODY MARY ALLA RESCHIO

*Serves 1*

2 LARGE RED BELL
PEPPERS

½ THUMB-SIZE PIECE
OF FRESH GINGER

A HINT OF BROWN
SUGAR (OPTIONAL)

FINE SEA SALT AND
FRESHLY GROUND
BLACK PEPPER

2 THIN SLICES
FRESH PEPERONCINO
OR OTHER
HOT CHILE PEPPER

1½ OUNCES / 45 ML
VODKA

ICE CUBES

1 SPRIG OF FRESH
MARJORAM, FOR
GARNISH

1 SPRIG OF FRESH
FENNEL FRONDS
(OPTIONAL),
FOR GARNISH

1 CELERY STALK,
FOR GARNISH

Think of a place. In a fairy tale. Somewhere you feel like you've been often before, but not quite. At once a familiar flavor and a completely new one. A classic revisited. Very much like the people that made it. Nencia and Benedikt Bolza, a Florentine princess and a Hungarian count. Two of the loveliest, most interesting people, devoted to a great piece of land in Umbria, developing it lovingly for their children and future generations. It's a very overused term, but visiting them makes me feel I've snuck into paradise, graced by their hospitality, immersing myself in the beauty of their lands, and this drink, a spicy, healthy, warming elixir that is so good, so friendly, so dangerous. This is a drink, or a riff on a drink, born from that place: made with peppers from their own synergic gardens; the original idea might not be local, but the approach couldn't be more so. Old-fashioned yet modern and chic, it's perfectly Italian.

1   In a juicer, juice the bell peppers and ginger according to the manufacturer's directions.

2   Pour into a glass and add the brown sugar (if using), a dash each of salt and black pepper, the peperoncino slices, and vodka. Stir well and add a few ice cubes.

3   Garnish with the marjoram, fennel fronds (if using), and celery. Drink immediately.

# PRAMPOLINI
## Red Wine Spritz

*Serves 1 or many*

ICE CUBES

2 PARTS BARBERA
D'ASTI OR OTHER
MEDIUM-BODIED
RED WINE

1 PART CAMPARI

1 PART ITALIAN
CITRUS SODA
(SUCH AS CEDRATA)

1 ORANGE SLICE,
FOR GARNISH

One of our favorite restaurants in Torino, Al Gatto Nero, has a house "welcome" drink that mixes vermouth with red wine. They serve it in a small glass without ice, but well chilled. I always liked this drink, so I was curious when we discovered the Prampolini in a pizzeria in Paris. The drink was created in Torino in the thirties by a Futurist painter, Enrico Prampolini. He called his drink the carousel of alcohol (*giostra d'alcol*) and used Cedrata (a brand of citrus soda), Barbera wine, and Campari. The inclusion of red wine distinguishes the Pramoplini from the other *apertivi*, which is why we find it fun to serve to guests. Originally, Mr. Prampolini intended his concoction to be served with two skewers, one with a cube of cheese, the other a cube of chocolate. It does sound like a very futuristic idea, but I have never tried it and may never do so.

In an ice-filled tumbler, combine the wine and Campari. Add the soda. Garnish with a slice of orange. Serve immediately.

THEY SAY THAT TORINO IS THE MOST FRENCH OF ALL THE ITALIAN cities, a city built for a French duke whose descendants would become the first kings of a united Italy. The Savoy family had gained lands in northern Italy and eventually decided to move their capital to Torino from Chambéry in eastern France. After centuries of gaining and losing ground, a mix of backroom negotiations and battlefield antics (with the help of national hero Giuseppe Garibaldi, who handed them the south on a silver platter) led to the Savoy family of Piemonte becoming the rulers of Italy, and Vittorio Emanuele II the first king of a unified country. In those days, the fashion for the aristocracy was to eat only French food, which was considered more elevated and refined than Italian food (all the early cookbooks in the royal library are on French cooking and even written in French). Over time, the refined French approach of the royals mixed with local traditions, a process made even richer by the unparalleled produce of the region.

Piemonte—which literally means "at the foot of the mountains"—has Alps to the north and west, the Mediterranean (Liguria) to the south, and neighboring Lombardia (and partially Emilia-Romagna) to the east. An absolute culinary dream setting, and the reason, along with French influences, that Piedmontese cuisine is probably the most sophisticated and varied in all of Italy.

With this overabundance of Piedmontese dishes, it's a strange contradiction that relatively few have found their way onto the "Best of" list of Italian cuisine. The outside world is much more familiar with the dishes of Rome, Bologna, Milano, and Napoli. Some of this may be explained by tourism and travel, as Piemonte has relatively few visitors apart from the oenotourists and the annual pilgrims who come for the white truffles of Alba. Exceptions that everybody knows are panna cotta and grissini (torinesi), the bread sticks found on every Italian table. Grissini were originally created in the palace of Torino for a sickly duke with digestive problems. Someone apparently believed that a fat loaf of bread was unfit for a slim duke whose tiny mouth was more suited to munching on a slender bread stick, whose figure was not unlike the duke's.

Piemonte is a region of wine, of nuts and chocolate, of cheese. But maybe more than anything, when it comes to cooking, it is a region of meat. Agnolotti, the local raviolis, are stuffed with a meat filling and often served with a meat sauce. Vitello tonnato, thin slices of cold veal served with a creamy tuna sauce. *Brasato*, beef braised for hours in local red wine, often Barolo. Then there is bollito misto (mixed boiled meats); *carne cruda*, which is as simple as it gets—raw meat, not ground but cut by hand; not to mention various offal dishes like the *finanziera*. The list is endless and endlessly rich. There are some interesting particularities, like bagna cauda, an emulsion of anchovies, garlic, and olive oil that is served warm and used as a dip for raw vegetables like peppers, fennel, celery, and carrots or cooked ones like artichokes and cauliflower. The cheeses of Piemonte are frequently used in cooking, like the famous Castelmagno, which is wonderful when melted into pasta sauces. In addition to various versions of agnolotti, the local pasta of Piemonte is the tagliolini, or *tajarin*, fine strands of fresh egg pasta traditionally served with a meat sauce, cheese, or vegetables.

Cuneo, the province south of Torino, is home to incredible treasures, like the famous hazelnuts of Piemonte. Among other things, they inspired gianduja, the local chocolate spread that is mixed with hazelnut paste, and, even more famously, Nutella, which is based on the same idea. Other treasures of the province are the white truffles of Alba in late autumn, the porcini mushrooms in early fall, and of course the Barolos and Barbarescos, the kings of Italian wine.

The story of Torino used to be that of the Risorgimento, the Italian unification of the regions, with the glory of the city cemented as the first capital of Italy. Later, the story of Torino became the story of Fiat, the industrial marvel of postwar Italy. Workers from all over, particularly the south, flocked to Torino for a better life, and for a while they found it. When Fiat cut back on its activities in the latter part of the last century, it created a certain vacuum in a city looking for a new identity. In recent years, Piemonte has risen as a mecca of food: The Slow Food movement was founded in the region, as was the movement's academy, which is only half an hour from Torino. Lavazza, the biggest coffee company in Italy, is from Torino, and the first Eataly, the food emporium, was founded here as well.

One more thing that Torino is particularly well known for is *aperitivo*, both the drink and the ceremony. *Aperitivo* is a little alcoholic drink you have before dinner. It is also the act of standing, or sitting down, at the bar with a drink and nibbles. Vermouth, the base of most *aperitivo* drinks, was first created here in the eighteenth century, quickly gained popularity, and now every café in the city rolls out their little appetizers between 5 and 6 o'clock. The system is, you buy a drink and we give you something to eat with it. Before you eat dinner.

We have met so many good people in Torino (understandably, since we live here now), but a perfect candidate for my good Italian in Piemonte is Andrea Vannelli, the owner of our favorite restaurant, Al Gatto Nero. Originally a Tuscan restaurant, it rose to fame in the middle of the last century as the chicest place in town, innovative for its time, and always elegant and excellent.

The wonderful thing is, they haven't changed much. Andrea has replaced his father, who had also replaced his own father many years before. The menu, which was modern and contemporary then, would now be described as classic. It's the most dignified, thoughtful establishment, a place that moves at a slow pace. Andrea is warm and considerate and always respectful, intimate yet keeps his distance. His face lights up when he talks about wine, and his staff has been there forever. It's the kind of restaurant where you don't look at the menu but discuss your desires with the waiter and pair them with what's in season. A master class of current turned classic. I sometimes wonder if we didn't really move to Torino just because of Al Gatto Nero.

More good Italians in Piemonte are the Vergnanos of Chieri, a lovely town in the hills of Torino and home to the family's Caffè Vergnano, the oldest coffee roaster in Italy. We met them some years ago, through food and coffee, and we are indebted to them for, at least partially, "the keys to the city." Carolina, the dynamic daughter, has so much energy we call it the "Vergnano factor," and her father, Franco, who loves cooking, invited us for a feast that included his famous risotto "alla Frenky," which we share in this book (see page 195).

# TUNA SALAD
## WITH GREEN BEANS AND MINT

*Serves 4*

5 LARGE EGGS

1 POUND / 450 G
HARICOTS VERTS,
TRIMMED

6 TABLESPOONS
EXTRA-VIRGIN
OLIVE OIL

3 TABLESPOONS
BALSAMIC VINEGAR

¼ TEASPOON
CELERY SALT

¼ TEASPOON
FRESHLY GROUND
BLACK PEPPER

12 OUNCES / 340 G
DRAINED CANNED
TUNA CHUNKS

A HANDFUL OF
FRESH MINT LEAVES,
FINELY CHOPPED

When we lived in Paris, during what now seems another lifetime, we found good Italian restaurants hard to come by. Always obsessed by finding the best, we tried and failed countless times until we had assembled a trusted handful of restaurants. They might not have been as good as the real thing (which simply means being in Italy), but they were good enough for a Parisian couple with a growing family who were dreaming of their next summer holiday in Italy. One of these places, on rue des Canettes, was called Chez Bartolo and had a nice atmosphere, pretty good pizza, and this salad that we always ordered, which is sort of Italian, I guess. Chez Bartolo was run by, we later found out, Egyptians who looked quite Italian in their white shirts. They had an elderly lady who handled accounts and a resident cat or two who always managed to escape our dogs. It was a Sunday place.

I usually make this salad on hot days when I'm in no mood to deal with boiling pots, the days when we have picnic-style meals of cold cuts, melons, and such. I prepare it on a large plate and line the ingredients up as beautifully as I can without mixing them: a circle of beans, a smaller circle of eggs, and so on. The mint and balsamic are key.

1   In a large saucepan, combine the eggs with water to cover by 1 inch / 2.5 cm. Cover and bring to a boil over high heat. When the water has reached a boil, cook for 6 minutes over medium heat. Drain and run under cold water until cool. Peel and finely chop the eggs.

2   Bring a pot of salted water to a boil over high heat. Add the haricots verts and cook until al dente, about 5 minutes. Drain and set aside to cool, then cut into ½-inch / 1.25 cm pieces.

3   In a small screw-top jar, shake together the olive oil, balsamic vinegar, celery salt, and pepper.

4   To assemble the salad, spoon the tuna into the center of a large shallow bowl. Form a ring around the tuna with the chopped eggs, then the green beans. Just before serving, sprinkle with mint and drizzle with the vinaigrette.

# TOMATO JAM
## FROM MIMÌ ALLA FERROVIA

In Napoli, it's easy to get lost in all the pizza hype, but Napoli has truly amazing trattorias with local seafood and dishes like Neapolitan ragù, Genovese sauce, and incredible pastries. One of my favorite such establishments is Mimì alla Ferrovia, a family trattoria run by two brothers, the Giuglianos. And now, yes, you guessed it, it's about to be taken over by the next generation; one of them, Salvatore, is already in charge of all the cooking. I actually came for the Genovese sauce (used on both pasta and meat), but a little starter that someone ordered at a nearby table caught my eye. A simple ricotta cheese with a delightful-looking red sauce. I was curious as it looked more like a dessert than a starter. Not so, said Salvatore Giugliano. It's an appetite opener, he claimed, the sauce or jam is made from the tomatoes of Vesuvio, with a hint of sugar. My appetite, in a place like that, is always wide open anyway, but the jam was fabulous, and so here it is in this book, a surprise inclusion. Use as a jam or sauce for pâtés, hams, and especially on ricotta cheese.

*Makes about
2 cups / 650 g*

2¼ POUNDS / 1 KG
TOMATOES

3½ CUPS / 700 G
SUGAR

1 Chop the tomatoes. Scoop out the pulp and seeds and reserve them in a bowl. Transfer the chopped tomatoes to a large bowl. Place the pulp and seeds in a fine-mesh sieve and press with a spoon. Add the strained pulp to the tomatoes. Discard the seeds.

2 Add the sugar to the tomatoes and pulp and let macerate, covered, for 2 hours.

3 Transfer to a large saucepan and set over low heat. Cook, uncovered and stirring occasionally, until thickened and glossy, about 45 minutes. Let cool and store in a jar in the refrigerator for up to 3 months.

# ROASTED PEPPER SALAD

*Serves 6*

3½ POUNDS / 1.5 KG
MIXED BELL PEPPERS
(ABOUT 8 PEPPERS)

8 OUNCES / 230 G
DAY-OLD COUNTRY
BREAD, CRUSTS
CUT OFF

3 GARLIC CLOVES,
THINLY SLICED

4 TABLESPOONS
EXTRA-VIRGIN
OLIVE OIL

FINE SEA SALT AND
FRESHLY GROUND
BLACK PEPPER

A HANDFUL OF
FRESH BASIL LEAVES,
FOR GARNISH

In Italian restaurants, it's very typical to order many different anti-pasti for the whole table rather than one per person. That way, everybody gets a bit of everything and more of what they like. This simple, light dish is perfect for such sharing, not necessarily tailored for one person, but wonderful when it shares the spotlight with various other foods and flavors.

1  Roast the peppers directly over a gas flame or under the broiler, turning occasionally, until charred all over, about 10 minutes. Transfer to a large bowl, cover tightly with plastic wrap, and let steam for 15 minutes. When cool enough to handle, peel and seed the peppers, then cut them into ½-inch / 1.25 cm strips.

2  Meanwhile, in a food processor, pulse the bread until it is finely chopped. Add the garlic and pulse until bread crumbs form; you should have about 1½ cups.

3  In a large nonstick skillet, heat 2 tablespoons of the olive oil. Add the bread crumbs and cook over medium-low heat, stirring frequently, until golden and crisp, about 5 minutes. Transfer the bread crumbs to paper towels and season with salt.

4  Wipe out the skillet. Add the remaining 2 tablespoons olive oil and heat over medium heat. Add the peppers and cook, stirring occasionally, until very tender, about 8 minutes. Season with salt and pepper.

5  Transfer the peppers to a large bowl or platter and garnish with the basil. Serve the bread crumb topping on the side, for sprinkling.

# INSALATA RUSSA ALLA MIMI

*Potato and Egg Salad*

I t's funny, but I grew up spending summers in the South of France eating a salad they called Salade Piémontaise. Then we moved to Piemonte, and the same salad here is called Insalata Russa. Whatever the origins, this lovely dish is very much part of the Piedmontese canon of starters, often served on its own and simply eaten with a fork as a first course. We rarely serve it that way, preferring to include it in a picnic-style meal or to greet guests who arrive too late for lunch and too early for dinner. A generous bowl of Insalata Russa, some *salumi*, pickles, a good loaf of bread—not to mention a bottle of well-chosen wine. I can't think of a warmer welcome.

1  Pour 1 inch / 2.5 cm water into a large pot and bring to a boil over high heat. Set a steamer insert in the pot and add the potatoes and carrot to the insert. Cover and reduce the heat to medium. Steam until the vegetables are firm-tender, 5 to 8 minutes. Add the peas 2 minutes before the end. Drain and let cool.

2  In a small bowl, stir together ½ teaspoon of salt and the mustard. Add the vinegar and stir well. Pour in the olive oil and continue to stir the vinaigrette vigorously.

3  In a large bowl, gently combine the steamed vegetables, diced tomato, and eggs. Add the chopped pickles and parsley. Fold in the mayonnaise and crème fraîche, mix gently, then pour in the vinaigrette. Mix everything together as gently as possible. Season with salt and pepper.

4  Cover the bowl with plastic wrap and refrigerate for at least 1 hour before serving.

*Serves 6*

2 LARGE POTATOES, PEELED AND CUT INTO SMALL DICE

1 LARGE CARROT, CUT INTO SMALL DICE

4 OUNCES / 110 G FRESH PEAS

FINE SEA SALT

1 TEASPOON DIJON MUSTARD

1 TABLESPOON RED WINE VINEGAR

2 TABLESPOONS EXTRA-VIRGIN OLIVE OIL

1 LARGE TOMATO, CUT INTO SMALL DICE

4 HARD-BOILED EGGS, PEELED AND CUT INTO SMALL DICE

6 OUNCES / 170 G SMALL AND FIRM PICKLES, FINELY CHOPPED

2 CUPS / 50 G FINELY CHOPPED FRESH PARSLEY LEAVES

½ CUP / 120 ML MAYONNAISE

¼ CUP / 60 ML CRÈME FRAÎCHE

FRESHLY GROUND BLACK PEPPER

# SAGE FRITTERS

*Makes 20 to
30 fritters,
depending on size*

2½ CUPS / 300 G
ALL-PURPOSE FLOUR

½ TEASPOON SUGAR

1 TEASPOON FINE
SEA SALT, PLUS MORE
FOR FINISHING

¼ TEASPOON GRATED
NUTMEG

1 CUP / 250 ML
ICE-COLD BLOND
LAGER BEER

LIGHT VEGETABLE
OIL, FOR
DEEP-FRYING
(ABOUT 1½ QUARTS /
LITERS)

20 TO 30 SAGE
LEAVES, DEPENDING
ON SIZE

When I host a large party (and hosting a large party can be a little stressful, even if I always try to entertain with ease), I like to hit the ground running. When guests arrive, they are served a well-chilled sparkling wine and then, boom, a piping hot, crunchy on the outside, slightly chewy on the inside, salty, flavorful sage fritter. After that, everything is easy. I have their hearts with reviews like "Oh my god, this is the best thing I've ever tasted" happening every time. I even think it's the best thing I've ever tasted when I make them. These fritters are universally popular, and they're vegetarian, so almost anyone can eat them. I use the freshest sage, usually that I've grown myself (sage is very easy to grow, unlike basil, which is more sensitive). I pick the largest leaves, lay a huge, freshly rinsed bunch on a white linen cloth (which looks beautiful), and start frying. When the first guests have had their fill, I sometimes deputize the willing into getting more sage and dipping, frying, and serving it. In return, they get to have more sage fritters.

1 Sift the flour into a large bowl. Add the sugar, salt, and nutmeg. Whisk in the beer until everything is combined and the mixture is thick enough to coat the back of a spoon.

2 Pour 1 inch / 2.5 cm oil into a large, high-sided pan. Heat the oil to about 375°F / 190°C. You can test if the oil is hot enough by adding in a small drop of batter: If it sizzles and turns golden and crisp, the oil is ready.

3 Working in batches and adding one at a time, dip the sage leaves into the batter, then fry, flipping frequently for even cooking, until crispy and golden, about 3 minutes.

4 Place the sage fritters on a large plate covered with paper towels to absorb the excess oil. Transfer to a serving plate, season with salt, and serve immediately.

# ZUCCHINI BLOSSOM FRITTERS STUFFED
## WITH MOZZARELLA AND ANCHOVIES

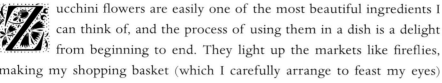 ucchini flowers are easily one of the most beautiful ingredients I can think of, and the process of using them in a dish is a delight from beginning to end. They light up the markets like fireflies, making my shopping basket (which I carefully arrange to feast my eyes) look like a still-life painting. At home, they brighten my kitchen for a brief moment before making every dish they belong to look beautiful. I try to get the biggest, perkiest, freshest flowers I can find, and one way to enjoy them is in these delicious fritters. You can either serve them with *aperitivo*, standing up, or include them in a sit-down meal before the *primi*.

*Makes 10 fritters*

½ CUP / 60 G
TIPO "00" FLOUR

½ TEASPOON FINE
SEA SALT, PLUS MORE
FOR SEASONING

¼ CUP / 60 ML
LUKEWARM
WHOLE MILK

2 LARGE EGGS

10 ZUCCHINI
BLOSSOMS

1 BALL (5 OUNCES /
150 G) MOZZARELLA
CHEESE, CUT INTO
10 PIECES
1½ INCHES /
4 CM LONG

5 GOOD-QUALITY
OIL-PACKED
ANCHOVY FILLETS,
HALVED

LIGHT VEGETABLE
OIL, FOR DEEP-
FRYING (ABOUT
1½ QUARTS /
LITERS)

1 In a medium bowl, combine the flour and salt. Add the milk and eggs and whisk to form a smooth batter, thick enough to coat the back of a spoon.

2 Gently open each zucchini blossom and remove the stamen. Wash gently and pat dry with a paper towel.

3 Stuff each flower with a piece of mozzarella and an anchovy. Gently fold the petals as if closing the blossom.

4 Pour 1 inch / 2.5 cm oil into a large, high-sided pan. Heat the oil to about 375°F / 190°C. You can test if the oil is hot enough by adding a small drop of batter: If it sizzles and turns golden and crisp, the oil is ready.

5 Working with one at a time, dip a blossom into the batter and add to the oil. Fry up to 4 blossoms at a time. Cook until crispy and golden, about 2 minutes on each side.

6 Place the zucchini blossom fritters onto a large plate covered with paper towels to absorb the excess oil. Transfer to a serving plate, season with salt, and serve immediately.

# FIORI DI ZUCCA RIPIENI

*Baked Zucchini Blossoms Stuffed with Prosciutto and Hazelnuts*

**Serves 6**

⅔ CUP / 150 G
WHOLE-MILK
ITALIAN-STYLE
RICOTTA CHEESE OR
DRAINED REGULAR
RICOTTA

6 SLICES PROSCIUTTO
DI PARMA, THINLY
SLICED CROSSWISE

⅓ CUP / 50 G
BLANCHED
HAZELNUTS, FINELY
CHOPPED

½ CUP / 50 G GRATED
PECORINO ROMANO
CHEESE

10 LEAVES FRESH
BASIL, FINELY
CHOPPED

FINE SEA SALT AND
FRESHLY GROUND
BLACK PEPPER

12 MEDIUM TO LARGE
ZUCCHINI BLOSSOMS

2 LARGE EGGS

2 TABLESPOONS
WHOLE MILK

1⅔ CUPS / 100 G
FRESH BREAD CRUMBS

EXTRA-VIRGIN
OLIVE OIL

1 LEMON, CUT
INTO WEDGES

For a long time, I made a version of stuffed zucchini flowers with ricotta and prosciutto. The problem was that while we all liked them, we always seemed to love the fried zucchini flower fritters (page 67) more, and this baked one felt a little limp and bland by comparison. But I'm not always in the mood to deep-fry, especially when it's hot or if I just polished the stove and don't want to spoil it yet. The solution came in the form of bread crumbs, which lend just the right amount of crunch for us to fall in love. While these breaded flowers don't really need anything more, adding a little bit of tomato sauce, even just to decorate the plate, elevates this dish, making it a little more cheffy and thus perfect for dinner parties.

1  Preheat the oven to 400°F / 200°C.

2  In a small bowl, mix the ricotta, prosciutto, hazelnuts, pecorino, and basil. Season with salt and pepper.

3  Carefully remove the stamen from the zucchini blossoms and rinse them. Drain and gently pat dry. Stuff the ricotta mixture inside the flowers, then tie them closed with kitchen twine, like a small bouquet.

4  In a shallow bowl, beat the eggs with the milk. Place the bread crumbs in a separate bowl. Drizzle a baking dish with olive oil. Dip each flower in the egg mixture and then into the bread crumbs. Place the stuffed flowers in the baking dish. Gently drizzle the flowers with olive oil (see Note).

5  Bake the flowers, turning them gently halfway through, until golden brown, about 20 minutes. Just before serving, sprinkle with salt and pepper, and serve with lemon wedges.

NOTE: *Use an olive oil spray instead of pouring from a bottle—much more efficient.*

# BAGNA CAUDA
## Garlic and Anchovy Dip Served with Raw Vegetables

This is probably the most polarizing dish in the book; people usually love or hate anchovies, and this dish takes it a few steps further. Bagna cauda is a pungent but delicious emulsion of anchovy and garlic that's served hot. Diners dip cut vegetables, such as peppers, cauliflower, celery, and carrots, and even meat and bread, into the mixture and rejoice.

A local tradition is to throw a bagna cauda party in late autumn when people gather for the sole purpose of enjoying an anchovy- and garlic-infused meal. As with most classic dishes, bagna cauda exists in various versions, but this one, from the very traditional Piedmontese restaurant Tre Galline in Torino, is the one I really fell in love with. I have it almost every week from November to late January. The head chef, Andrea Chiuni, graciously lent me his recipe; I guess after all my visits to the restaurant, he saw how much it meant to me.

1   Place the anchovies in a bowl; cover with the red wine. Set aside for an hour at room temperature.

2   Combine the garlic, the olive oil, and 6 tablespoons (90 g) of the butter in a saucepan. Heat the pan on a very low heat, making sure not to brown the garlic. Cook the garlic until tender, about an hour.  Once softened, crush the garlic with a fork (or you can use an immersion blender). Drain the anchovies and add to the garlic mixture, crushing them with a fork. Continue to cook on a very low heat for 3 hours, stirring occasionally, until you get a textured sauce. Remove from the heat and add the remaining butter and the vinegar and stir. Allow the sauce to cool for 5 minutes, stirring continuously.

3   Traditionally bagna cauda sauce is served in a terra cotta pot called a *fojot* with a candle inside to keep the emulsion hot, but you can re-create this with a small fondue pot. Serve with raw sliced vegetables, such as bell peppers, cardoons, cauliflower, radicchio, cabbage, celery, broccoli, Jerusalem artichokes, baby artichokes, and endives. It's also delicious with a few boiled potatoes. At Tre Galline, they also serve raw meats like beef and the local Bra sausage.

*Serves 8*

8 OUNCES / 240 G ANCHOVY FILLETS, PREFERABLY PRESERVED IN SALT, RINSED AND DEBONED

½ CUP / 120 ML RED WINE (AT TRE GALLINE, THEY USE BARBERA)

24 MEDIUM CLOVES GARLIC, PEELED AND HALVED

½ CUP / 120 ML OLIVE OIL

½ CUP / 120 G UNSALTED BUTTER

1 TEASPOON RED WINE VINEGAR

FRESH VEGETABLES, FOR SERVING

# TORTINO DELLA VALLE GRANA

## Poached Pears with Radicchio and Castelmagno Cheese

*Serves 4*

2 HEADS RADICCHIO

2 TABLESPOONS EXTRA-VIRGIN OLIVE OIL

FINE SEA SALT

2 TABLESPOONS / 30 G UNSALTED BUTTER

3 PEARS IN SYRUP (RECIPE FOLLOWS), DRAINED AND EACH CUT INTO 3 OR 4 PIECES

1 TEASPOON SAFFRON THREADS

8 OUNCES / 230 G CASTELMAGNO CHEESE (SEE NOTE), CRUMBLED

NOTE: *If you can't get Castelmagno cheese, replace it with a tasty blue cheese that crumbles well, like Stilton.*

In the Piedmontese countryside, about an hour south of Torino, is a magical estate called Tenuta il Palazzasso. It's one of the most beautiful houses I have ever visited, majestic rooms filled with beauty and curiosities. Some of the magic, however, comes not from the perfectly painted wallpapers or the ornate furniture, but from the people who live there. Our friends Andrea and Chicca, the loveliest couple you'll ever meet, decided several years ago to move full time to what was traditionally the family's summer palace. They are involved in local farming, and their dream is to bring the place back to bustling life, just like in the old days when it was a self-sustaining, noble property. I love spending time there, just me and Oddur for a bit of romance, or with all the kids for . . . less romance. Whenever we do, I beg Chicca to make this little starter (so delicious and representative of this part of Piemonte) of local pears and the famous Castelmagno cheese, which is only made in the mountainous valley that stretches from nearby Caraglio in the direction of the French border.

1 Cut the radicchio heads into quarters. Cut out and discard the core from each quarter, and cut the quarters into bite-size pieces.

2 In a large sauté pan, heat the olive oil over medium heat. Add the radicchio and a pinch of salt. Cook, stirring occasionally, until tender, about 5 minutes. Set aside.

3 In the same pan, heat the butter over medium heat. Add the pears and saffron and cook until hot and coated in butter, about 2 minutes.

4 Place a 3.9 inch / 10 cm ring mold (2 inches / 5 cm deep) in the center of an individual serving plate. Make a layer of radicchio, using a spoon to press everything into place, then add a layer of pears. Remove the ring gently so nothing falls out of place, and scatter some crumbled cheese on top. Repeat for remaining servings. It is important to serve this dish as hot as possible so the cheese melts on top of the pears.

## Pears in Syrup
### *Makes 6 pears*

6 RIPE MADERNASSA PEARS (SEE NOTE)

JUICE OF 1 LEMON

3 WHOLE CLOVES

3 CUPS / 600 G SUGAR

1 CINNAMON STICK

1  Peel and halve the pears. Core the pears
   to hollow out a nice round shape in the
   center of the fruit.

2  In a saucepan large enough to contain the
   pears, combine the pears, 2 cups / 500 ml
   water, the lemon juice, cloves, sugar,
   and cinnamon stick. Bring to a boil over
   medium heat and cook until the sugar has
   completely dissolved, 15 to 20 minutes.
   Remove from the heat and let cool. Stored
   in an airtight container with their syrup,
   the pears will last up to 5 days in the
   refrigerator.

NOTE: *You can use any type of pear here.*

# NOTES ON THE ITALIAN RESTAURANT

## Oddur Thorisson

IMAGINE YOU'RE SOMEWHERE IN ITALY. It's around noon and you're hungry. You are looking for a good place to eat, and someone gave you the name of a restaurant worth checking out. You turn into a side street, a little alley. The street is empty. Maybe you pass a cat or an old Vespa leaning up against a rosy terra-cotta wall. From the outside, the restaurant looks like any other, a nice enough storefront, not touristy, the sign is pretty. Trattoria something or other, ristorante this or that. Perhaps, if it's the right time of year, there are some inviting tables outside.

The inside is not striking, but it's pleasant, classic, simple, which can be, and often is, more striking than . . . striking. There are bottles of wine on wooden shelves (which for a wine lover is slightly alarming—all that hot wine aging badly—but you'll overlook it because it's beautiful), a little booth or a desk where a signora of a certain age is ready to take your payment after lunch. Everything is unsurprising, and that's a good thing. There are some signs that this establishment is more upscale than down—white tablecloths and napkins, a bit more silver with a bit more shine. The waiters could be wearing white jackets and black bow ties. If they are, you are probably in a city or a historical holiday place, somewhere the jet-setters used to go and maybe still do.

It's quite likely that close to the entrance you'll find a display of antipasti and some exciting seasonal ingredients. So fresh looking and appetizing that they're already playing with your mind and your imminent order. Salads, anchovies, stuffed peppers, beautiful artichokes in spring, porcini in autumn, that sort of stuff. As you take your seat, you catch a glimpse of the final page, the last act, the dessert cart. You purr at the notion of choosing anything you want from there, but you don't want to. Not yet—you want to enjoy the show first. And make no mistake, it is a show.

The likable, elegant waiter suggests a little glass of sparkling to start and you happily oblige. You run your fingers over the menu. No surprises there. The waiter returns with the wine and a little plate of something nice. Maybe culatello. He wants you to know that he's happy to add truffles to almost anything you like, and you nod but don't necessarily go for it. Let's say you decide on some porcini carpaccio, then a risotto. After that, how about the pigeon? You lean back in your seat, you take a second look at the dessert cart. You measure what's there against what you've ordered. You wonder if it's obscene to have two desserts.

The question you have to ask yourself now is simple: "Is there any other place, anywhere in the world that you would rather be?"

Everyone knows that you can eat well in Italy. Everywhere. You could be driving in a region you don't know, into a village you've never heard of, and if it's a big enough village to have a place to eat, the food will most likely be good and certainly edible. Maybe not stunning, but absolutely fine and probably better than that. A good plate of pasta, thinly sliced veal, tiramisù. A glass of wine. Done. We take this for granted but shouldn't. It's a miracle that exists in no other country in the world. I can't say for sure why, but I have my suspicions that the explanation lies, like so much else in this country, in one word. *Famiglia.*

Nonna and Nonno had a place and now he's in a frame on the wall, but she's still cooking away, albeit more slowly than before. Their son is in the front room taking orders and telling jokes. Some nights his wife might be there, too, adding up bills; and even their little ones might be running around, gently toying with guests. It's not that the son, let's call him Franco, never thought about leaving. This isn't necessarily his dream job. But he likes it, or at least doesn't hate it, and his mother needs him. And he likes his village enough to stay. He also might not know what else to do. If he lacks the funds to overhaul the look of the place (or has the savvy *not to*), we have a recipe for a good, clean, well-run, traditional restaurant. And while there isn't much novelty in the cuisine, it's well executed and the ingredients are good. The same story would almost certainly not happen in France. As soon as Papa was gone, the son would have his mother sell the bistrot and move to Paris or someplace else in search of the American dream. And who would be the buyer? A local businessman, someone who already owns three other joints selling kebabs and pizzas.

A place like this can't be taken for granted. I fear it may not always exist. Globalization. The dangerous word that is positive on the face of it and supposed to make the world a harmonious place. Making every Main Street on the planet identical, everybody speaking English, living through their phones, making a homogenous tribe out of us all.

A really special restaurant is almost impossible to create quickly. It needs time. It needs, in cooking terms, to sit. The longer, the better. A concept is a clever idea that someone had. A great restaurant has its own ideas, evolving organically over time, and Italy is full of places like that.

When I visit friends in what they call "major cities," they usually have lined up for us the best places, the most happening, the awesome. And next time we come, they have new awesomes. It's about ticking things off a list: Go there once, then go someplace else. Never be caught dead in last week's world. Now "there" is somewhere else. Not better but newer.

A real restaurant needs regulars. No place that requires anyone to reserve three months in advance will ever have those. The staff won't stay. They, too, will go on to the next big thing. Like rats from a sinking ship, they know before anyone that it won't last. Something more exciting is around the corner. Except it's not.

You could break restaurants down into roughly three categories. First, those that exist for money. That's most of them. None of those are ever any good. They will feed you, sometimes almost satisfy. Almost. But most of them are appalling. I try not to ever go to any of those.

Then there is the restaurant that exists for glory. Only glory. Michelin stars, accolades.

That's a scary thought. The chef that's cooking for the mind, not the mouth. And not even *your* mind, but the mind of critics who "understand" conceptual cooking, like the Emperor's New Clothes. There are exceptions. Very good exceptions. But they are few—much like any other art form. And cooking can be art. Of course, Italy has many of those, but good or bad, they are international rather than Italian and are not what I mean when I talk about the Italian restaurant.

Then there is my favorite. The real thing. A place that wouldn't mind making money. Or getting some good reviews. But they live in the third dimension. They just are. Because they are. A lot of Italian restaurants are like that.

A great restaurant is not necessarily the same as a great chef. Nobody doubts the cooking skills of some of the world's leading chefs. But the setup means that people go there once. Or a few times at the most. Until the chef closes and comes up with a fresher concept. It's more about an experience than just eating out, about discovery more than delight. When it works, it really works, but the problem is that for the few geniuses, there are legions of imitators. Ones where you have to wait three months for a table and sit four hours

through a meal where your conversational mojo is constantly being interrupted by long-winded food explanations. And then you have to pay the price of several good meals. It had better be worth it. And not just because you can now tick it off the list or tell your friends you went there. Worth it because it was.

A truly good restaurant needs regulars. A healthy dose of "your usual table" or "your favorite is back on the menu, sir." It's surprising, but a restaurant that always has a fresh crowd becomes strangely stale, like a hit show without a soul. People, not only food, make the best places. And sometimes they need to be the same people.

Imagine you are somewhere in Italy. It's around noon and you're hungry. You are looking for a good place to eat and you know where to go. They know your name and your appetites and your favorite place to sit. They bring the *aperitivo* you like and one day you don't even need to glance at the dessert cart. You know what's on it. And you know what you'll take. They know it, too. And if the place is crowded, there's a chance that someone else might want it, too, so they'll save you a slice. A place that saves you a slice, that's the Italian restaurant.

# ASPARAGUS
## Steamed Asparagus with Parmesan Butter Sauce

*Serves 4*

2 POUNDS / 900 G
ASPARAGUS, WOODY
ENDS TRIMMED

4 TABLESPOONS /
60 G UNSALTED
BUTTER, MELTED
AND KEPT WARM

½ CUP / 40 G
GRATED PARMESAN
CHEESE

2 HARD-BOILED
EGGS, PEELED AND
FINELY CHOPPED

FINE SEA SALT

ot only is asparagus one of my favorite foods, but I think it's one of the healthiest and most life-lengthening. Asparagus season coincides with the months just before bathing-suit season, which is perfect timing as it's so rich and filling while still lean and light on the hips. From February to May, I have asparagus every day, and while we most often have it blanched to al dente perfection with just olive oil and lemon, this is a more indulgent version, a little more festive, and definitely a little bit more delicious.

1   Set up a bowl of ice and water. Pour 1 inch / 2.5 cm of water into a pot. Place the asparagus in a steamer insert and the insert in the pot. Cover and set over high heat. Once steam forms, cook until bright green and fork-tender, 3 to 4 minutes. Shock in the ice water bath to stop cooking. Drain well.

2   In a small bowl, combine the warm melted butter and the Parmesan. Place the asparagus on a serving plate and drizzle the butter sauce all over. Scatter with the chopped eggs, season with salt, and serve immediately.

# EGGPLANT PARMIGIANA

One of the most famous antipasti, cooked around the world, eggplant Parmigiana exists in various versions, sizes, and shapes and is claimed by not one but two regions as their local treasure. I don't really know whom to believe, Napoli or Sicily, but it's worth remembering that they were once the same kingdom, and thus the lines are blurred. Besides, a well-made Parmigiana is so great that it can easily be shared by two different places and make them both proud. In restaurants, I tend to order a Parmigiana at the beginning of a meal, which is the traditional way, but at home, we play around a little bit more and sometimes serve it alongside meat, or even on its own as a main course, especially if we had a big *aperitivo* earlier in the night.

1  Cut the eggplants lengthwise into slices ½ inch / 1.25 cm thick and sprinkle them with salt. Set aside for 30 minutes, then rub away the excess salt with paper towels.

2  Preheat the oven to 400°F / 200°C.

3  In a large skillet, heat ½ cup of the olive oil over medium-high heat. Working in batches, fry the eggplant slices until golden on each side, about 3 minutes. Place them on paper towels to drain the excess oil. Set aside.

4  Meanwhile, in a medium saucepan, heat the remaining 2 tablespoons olive oil over medium heat. Add the garlic and onion and sauté until translucent, about 3 minutes. Add the passata, a pinch of salt, and the basil leaves. Cover and cook on low until the tomato sauce is thickened, 10 to 15 minutes.

5  Pour a ladle of the tomato sauce into a 9 × 13-inch / 23 × 33 cm baking dish. Build layers in this order: fried eggplant, tomato sauce, Parmesan, and mozzarella. Repeat the process, ending with a layer of tomato sauce and Parmesan.

6  Bake until bubbling and golden brown, about 25 minutes. Let sit at room temperature for 10 minutes, then serve.

*Serves 4 to 6*

4 MEDIUM EGGPLANTS

FINE SEA SALT

½ CUP / 120 ML PLUS 2 TABLESPOONS EXTRA-VIRGIN OLIVE OIL

1 GARLIC CLOVE, THINLY SLICED

1 SMALL ONION, THINLY SLICED

2½ CUPS / 600 ML TOMATO PASSATA (STRAINED PUREE OF RAW TOMATOES)

10 FRESH BASIL LEAVES

⅔ CUP / 60 G FINELY GRATED PARMESAN CHEESE

7 OUNCES / 200 G MOZZARELLA CHEESE, SLICED

# CAPONATA DI MELANZANE
## FROM FABRIZIA LANZA
### Eggplant Caponata

*Serves 8 to 10*

1 HEAD CELERY,
TOUGH OUTER STALKS
DISCARDED AND
STRINGS REMOVED,
COARSELY SLICED

VEGETABLE OIL,
FOR FRYING

2 POUNDS / 1 KG
EGGPLANT, PEELED
AND CUT INTO
1-INCH / 2.5 CM CUBES

FINE SEA SALT

¼ CUP / 60 ML
EXTRA-VIRGIN
OLIVE OIL

1 LARGE ONION,
SLICED

6 OUNCES / 170 G
GREEN OLIVES (¾ TO
1 CUP), PITTED AND
COARSELY CHOPPED

4 TABLESPOONS
CAPERS, RINSED AND
DRAINED

1½ CUPS / 350 ML
TOMATO SAUCE

1 TABLESPOON SUGAR,
OR MORE TO TASTE

¼ CUP / 60 ML RED
WINE VINEGAR

8 HARD-BOILED EGGS,
PEELED AND HALVED,
FOR GARNISH

Having enjoyed it cooked in so many styles and forms throughout the years, I believe caponata is one of those iconic Italian dishes that's more an idea than a single recipe. Of course, all these variations share most of the same ingredients, but the cooking and presentations can diverge greatly. Earlier in this book, I professed my intention, for the sake of authenticity and quality, to seek out Italians I admire for advice and guidance, to compare notes, to learn from them, to broaden my horizon. One of those people is Fabrizia Lanza, who runs a wonderful cooking school that her mother started in the heartlands of Sicily. She is so dedicated to her beautiful project, so knowledgeable and interested in the subject of authentic Sicilian food. I loved spending a few precious days at her place, and I'm honored to borrow her recipe for caponata. With a little crunch and a lot of freshness, this version is more of a salad than some, which can be almost stew-like.

1   Fill a large bowl with ice and water. Bring a medium pot of water to a boil over medium heat. Plunge the sliced celery into the boiling water and cook briefly until al dente and still crisp, just 3 minutes. Drain and place in the ice water until chilled. Drain again and set aside.

2   Pour 1 inch / 2.5 cm of vegetable oil into a large sauté pan. Heat over medium-high heat. Working in batches, fry the eggplant cubes until browned, about 3 minutes. Drain well on paper towels. Season with salt.

3   In a separate skillet, heat the olive oil over medium-high heat. Add the onion and sauté until just golden, about 5 minutes. Add the celery, olives, capers, tomato sauce, sugar, vinegar, and salt to taste. Gently stir in the eggplant, being careful not to break it up. Simmer for 2 to 3 minutes to combine, then transfer to a large bowl or platter to cool.

4   Pile the caponata in a pyramid and surround it with hard-boiled eggs. Serve cold or at room temperature.

# CARCIOFI ALLA GIUDIA
## *Jewish-Style Artichokes*

*Serves 6*

2 LEMONS,
QUARTERED

24 SMALL ROUND
ARTICHOKES, OR
6 LARGER ONES

FINE SEA SALT AND
FRESHLY GROUND
BLACK PEPPER

1½ QUARTS / LITERS
EXTRA-VIRGIN
OLIVE OIL

On our honeymoon in Rome twelve years ago, we discovered Piperno, a family restaurant that oozes old-school glamour. All the waiters look cast for a 1950s movie, every detail visually perfect without trying to be. No trip to Rome is complete without at least one visit, and on every visit, I order not one but two fried artichokes, which I refuse to share. When I thought of the recipes for this book, this was one of the very first I included on my list. Getting the recipe, however, was a little trickier than I expected. The Boni family are wonderful hosts, nice people, and eager to share, but they also like to keep their secrets. So we played a little game. On a recent visit, I placed my order and we had a discussion. Instead of them handing out the recipe, I asked questions, guessed, and they confirmed or denied—all very mysterious. I think this recipe is very close to the Piperno version; I've tried it many times and the results are lovely.

1   Fill a large bowl with water and add the lemon quarters. Remove the thickest layer of leaves from the artichokes and trim the stems. Place them upside down in the water and let soak for 15 minutes.

2   Drain the artichokes, pat dry, and season with salt and pepper.

3   Pour 2 to 3 inches / 5 to 7 cm of oil into a large saucepan. Heat the oil to about 280°F / 140°C over medium heat. Working in batches, add the artichokes and cook until nearly golden, about 10 minutes for small artichokes, 15 minutes for larger ones.

4   Using a slotted spoon, transfer the artichokes to a plate lined with paper towels. Let stand until cool enough to handle. Using your hands, open up the artichokes gently, like flowers. For larger artichokes, pull out and discard the fuzzy chokes.

5   Increase the oil temperature to 350°F / 180°C. Return the artichokes to the oil and fry until golden brown, up to 5 minutes longer. Drain on paper towels and season with salt and pepper. Serve immediately.

# TORTA PASQUALINA
*Chard and Egg Easter Pie*

## Serves 8

12 OUNCES / 350 G
SWISS CHARD,
WELL RINSED

6 LARGE EGGS

½ ONION, FINELY
DICED

1 CUP / 225 G
WHOLE-MILK
ITALIAN-STYLE
RICOTTA CHEESE OR
DRAINED REGULAR
RICOTTA

½ CUP / 50 G GRATED
PARMESAN CHEESE

¼ CUP / 20 G
GRATED PECORINO
ROMANO CHEESE

FINE SEA SALT AND
FRESHLY GROUND
BLACK PEPPER

½ TEASPOON GRATED
NUTMEG

TWO 9-INCH / 23 CM
ROLLED PIE CRUSTS
(8 OUNCES /
230 G EACH)

 ne of my favorite savory pies, and a great way to cook Swiss chard, is this traditional Easter cake that originates from Liguria but has traveled all over Italy and is now eaten in many households on Easter Sunday. I must confess that I have this pie year-round; like some of the other recipes in this chapter, it makes for wonderful picnic food and can be prepared ahead of time. For the sake of beauty, I take extra care to place the eggs with precision so each slice has a bright little moon in the middle.

1  Preheat the oven to 350°F / 180°C.

2  Bring a large pot of water to a boil over medium-high heat. Add the chard and cook for 3 minutes. Drain and squeeze out as much water as possible. Transfer to a cutting board and finely chop.

3  In a large bowl, combine 2 of the eggs, the onion, ricotta, Parmesan, and Pecorino Romano. Add the chard and mix all the ingredients together. Season with salt and pepper. Add the nutmeg.

4  Roll out 1 round of dough on a lightly floured work surface to a 10½-inch / 26 cm round about ⅛ inch / 3 mm thick. Transfer to a parchment-lined baking sheet. Roll out the remaining round of dough to the same size and thickness and carefully transfer to a 10-inch / 25 cm tart pan with a removable bottom. Press the dough firmly into the sides and bottom of the pan. Trim the excess dough, leaving about a ½-inch / 1.25 cm overhang. In a small bowl, beat 1 of the eggs to blend and brush the edges of the dough.

5  Scrape the chard mixture into the tart shell and spread evenly.

6  With the help of a spoon, gently create 3 little nests. Crack the remaining 3 eggs into the nests. Cover the pie with the second pastry round and seal the edges with the egg wash. Re-roll the remaining dough and cut out leaves or any of your favorite figures to decorate the tart. Place on top of the tart. Brush the surface with the egg wash.

7  Bake until golden brown, 40 to 50 minutes. Let cool for at least 2 hours before serving. It's even better served the next day.

# OVEN-BAKED EGGS
## WITH BOTTARGA AND PARSLEY

I so love eggs that, in fact, I get the jitters when I see our egg reserves go below the safety limit, which in my case is about two dozen. It's somehow primal in me, as if I think to myself, come hell or high water, as long as we have eggs everything will be all right. This dish, which is really cooking without cooking—what once would have been called a "bachelor dish" or "the ultimate midnight snack"—demonstrates perfectly how indispensable, versatile, and elegant eggs really are. This is really just a fried egg, but with enough finesse and flavor to open a meal and set the diner off in the right direction with its subtle flavors and textures, its hint of the sea. Eggs *en cocotte* are very French, but I have decided that the sprinkle of bottarga makes them Italian.

*Serves 4*

8 LARGE EGGS

FINE SEA SALT AND
FRESHLY GROUND
BLACK PEPPER

2 TABLESPOONS
EXTRA-VIRGIN
OLIVE OIL

¼ CUP / 50 G
GRATED BOTTARGA

2 TABLESPOONS
CHOPPED FRESH
PARSLEY

1  Preheat the oven to 350°F / 180°C.

2  Place four 6-inch / 15 cm ovenproof ramekins or flameproof baking dishes in the preheated oven for 10 minutes.

3  Meanwhile, crack 2 eggs into each of 4 small bowls. Season with salt and pepper.

4  Take out the hot ramekins. To each ramekin, add ½ tablespoon olive oil, then 2 eggs.

5  Turn the broiler on. Broil the eggs until the whites are set but the yolks are runny, 2 to 4 minutes.

6  To serve, top with grated bottarga and chopped parsley. Season with a hint of salt and pepper. Serve immediately.

# VITELLO TONNATO
## *Thinly Sliced Veal with Tuna Sauce*

*Serves 8*

*VEAL*

1 POUND 5 OUNCES /
600 G VEAL
SHOULDER

1 CARROT, COARSELY
CHOPPED

1 ONION, HALVED
BUT NOT PEELED

1 CELERY STALK,
COARSELY CHOPPED

2 GARLIC CLOVES,
PEELED AND LEFT
WHOLE

5 WHOLE CLOVES

6 BLACK
PEPPERCORNS

2 BAY LEAVES

PINCH OF FINE
SEA SALT

2 CUPS / 475 ML
WHITE WINE

ew dishes are more purely Piedmontese than this curious combination of thinly sliced veal and creamy tuna-flavored sauce. Vitello tonnato seems to have evolved over a long period through various experiments of flavoring meat with fish, such as tuna or anchovies, even treating the veal like tuna, salting and storing it in oil. The breakthrough seems to have come with the addition of mayonnaise, which increased the popularity of the dish and now seems to be the "official version" (although some purists refer to the older, mayonnaise-less recipe as the true vitello tonnato).

I had been making a version I liked for years before moving to Piemonte, but I must admit the move has upped my game considerably. Almost every restaurant in Torino and the Piedmontese countryside has a take on this dish, and each is the ultimate.

1  **Marinate the veal:** In a large saucepan, combine the veal, carrot, onion, celery, garlic, cloves, peppercorns, bay leaves, and salt. Pour the white wine over the top, cover, and let marinate at room temperature for 30 minutes.

2  Add 6 cups / 1.5 liters water to the pan. Bring to a boil, then immediately remove from the heat. Cover and let cool in the liquid for 2 hours.

3  **Meanwhile, make the tonnato sauce:** In a food processor, combine the tuna, capers, anchovy fillets, and egg yolks and blitz for about 30 seconds. Add the lemon juice and blitz for another 10 seconds. Season with black pepper.

4  With the food processor running, slowly add the olive oil in a single stream. The finished sauce will have a consistency similar to fresh mayonnaise.

5  To serve, remove the veal from the cooking liquid (discard the vegetables and herbs). Slice the veal as thinly as possible and place the slices on a large serving dish. Pour the sauce over the meat and garnish with the caperberries. Serve immediately.

## TONNATO SAUCE

4 OUNCES / 110 G
CANNED TUNA IN
OLIVE OIL, DRAINED

2 OUNCES / 60 G
CAPERS, DRAINED

4 OIL-PACKED
ANCHOVY FILLETS

4 LARGE HARD-
BOILED EGG YOLKS

JUICE OF ½ LEMON

FRESHLY GROUND
BLACK PEPPER

⅔ CUP / 160 ML
EXTRA-VIRGIN
OLIVE OIL

1½ TABLESPOONS
CAPERBERRIES,
DRAINED, FOR
GARNISH

MORE THAN ANY OTHER REGION IN ITALY (WITH SICILY PERHAPS THE only other candidate), Abruzzo feels like a country inside a country. There's the contrast of its tall, imposing mountains and their mountainous plains, which remind me of Iceland, with the greenest, most giving farmlands and beaches with their fish, meat, and vegetables. It is also, in some ways, one of the least "Italian" parts of Italy. Or rather, let's just say that this is not the Italy you'd find in Napoli or Rome, but rather a universe of farmers, sheepherders, and fishermen. Long an impoverished region, it was used by its more prosperous neighbors, like Lombardia, much like a kitchen garden (similar to the role Ireland used to play for England). The Abruzzese cultivated the finest saffron but used none of it themselves. It was too valuable and thus more or less all of it ended up in the golden risottos of the richer Milanese, rather than in their own regional dishes. They grew some of the best olives, but those, too, were shipped to Tuscany or Umbria and pressed there as local olive oil. Of course, like other regions, they always made delicious dishes, but it was hearty, nourishing fare, made without exotic or expensive ingredients—which, as it happens, is often the best cooking.

In recent years, the Abruzzese have fought back and reclaimed their produce, becoming a force within the Slow Food movement. Olive oil from Abruzzo is now as respected as if it came from Tuscany or Umbria, and some of the saffron never leaves home. The cuisine of Abruzzo is incredibly varied, much like its produce, and quite different from the rest of Italy, as the mountains long shielded it from outside influences.

The meat most commonly used is lamb and the most distinctive meat recipe of Abruzzo is grilled lamb skewers. The local pasta is called *spaghetti alla chitarra,* strands of fresh egg pasta made by pressing the dough through a guitar-like tool. This is often served with a tomato-based meat sauce or a tomato sauce that includes tiny little meatballs, which is very uncharacteristic for Italy but common in the United States—it's the only example in the country where meatballs are served with pasta (or at least the only one I can think of). Regional specialties include stuffed pancakes and a bouillabaisse-esque (I had to write it that way, couldn't resist) fish stew or soup, the *brodetto,* with a touch of spice. It's a cuisine of surf and turf, if one can still use such an expression. And that's not to mention the desserts, such as the waffle-like wafers called pizzelle or the delicious *bocconotti* stuffed with almonds and chocolate. Some of the desserts and sweets have even spread all over Italy.

Leading the Abruzzo food revolution is one of my good Italians, master chef Niko Romito. A holder of three Michelin stars, he is widely considered a culinary genius and one of the absolute best chefs in Italy today. In addition to his flagship restaurant, which he runs with his sister, Cristiana, he's involved in several ambitious projects in his hometown of Castel di Sangro to preserve the traditions of the region. He recently opened a new eatery concept, ALT (meaning "stop" in Italian); it's situated on a busy freeway and meant to serve as an alternative for locals and passersby who want a quick bite, but an absolutely delicious one, like the most delicious fried chicken you'll ever have. A project I am particularly fascinated by is his work with a group of hospitals. Realizing they were on a shoestring budget, he didn't urge them to increase their spending or buy different ingredients. Instead, he pragmatically said, "Send me what you always buy and let's see what we can do with it."

We have mixed feelings about Michelin restaurants, but dining at Niko's is a revelation. Everything is so incredibly thought out, yet the outcome is so simple. It's the difference between being elevated and trying to seem like you're elevated. A show with substance.

Niko agreed to share a recipe for this book, and while most of his cooking is not exactly accessible, we thought it was essential to include at least one of his creations. In reading this book, you will notice that we are very concerned with preserving traditions. At the same time, I realize that things can't ever stand completely still. A restaurant that is run without vigor, ambition, and a healthy dose of enterprise becomes a dull museum, even if it's a beautiful one. Being at Niko's makes me feel like I have one foot in the past, the other in the future.

Our other good Italians here are the Pepe family in northern Abruzzo, very close to the borders of Marche. Emidio, the patriarch, has been making wine since the '60s. Bottled wine for aging, that is; the family had always made wine before, but for immediate consumption. Emidio, who looks like an Italian winemaker in a Hollywood movie, was the first one who believed in the indigenous grapes of the region, enough to stake his family's future on them. I was particularly moved by the story of how he first sold his wines in the United States, arriving in New York with his bottles in a suitcase and showing up, without much knowledge of English, at the doors of restaurateurs. Lidia Bastianich proved a great ally, and translator. It was still illegal to transport alcohol across state lines, and a good story, or at least a funny image, is of him hiding under a bridge with a trunk full of wine while the cops drove overhead. Emidio is a sharp dresser, stylish, and oddly fashionable. In the early days, he couldn't afford to attend the biggest wine fair in Italy, but once he could, he bought himself a new suit to wear to the fair that year, and then a new suit every year after that. It sounds trivial but also tells of such discipline and respect, for his wine, his buyers, for himself, and his family.

Now, the winery is largely run by his daughters and granddaughter, but when we first arrived, he was, at eighty-six, busy planting fava beans in the field. We had not planned to stay, but couldn't bear to leave. A few more seats were added to the table and a few more bottles opened.

# SCARPETTA
## *Lamb Pâté with Bread Soaked in Lamb Jus*

*Serves 4*

*LAMB PÂTÉ*

3 TABLESPOONS /
45 G UNSALTED
BUTTER

1 SPRIG OF FRESH
THYME

1 SPRIG OF
FRESH SAGE

1 SPRIG OF FRESH
ROSEMARY

1 SPRIG OF FRESH
MARJORAM

9 OUNCES / 250 G
BONELESS LAMB
SHOULDER, CHOPPED
INTO LARGE CHUNKS

9 OUNCES / 250 G
LAMB LIVER,
CHOPPED

¾ CUP / 200 ML
MONTEPULCIANO DI
ABRUZZO TULLUM
RED WINE (FEUDO
ANTICO) OR ANY
FULL-BODIED RED
WINE, IDEALLY FROM
ABRUZZO

½ TABLESPOON RED
WINE VINEGAR

1 TEASPOON FINE
SEA SALT

½ TEASPOON
COLATURA DI ALICI
(ANCHOVY EXTRACT)

This is a dish layered with meaning. Niko Romito (whom I mentioned in the essay on Abruzzo on page 95) is considered one of the finest chefs in Italy. This dish is a love letter to his native Abruzzo and a very interesting take on the Italian tradition of *fare la scarpetta*, which translates to "make the little shoe"—with the little shoe being that small piece of bread you use to mop up the last bit of sauce or soup. Niko's *scarpetta* is a variation on this theme, but it uses ingredients native to Abruzzo, like Montepulciano wine and lamb, in addition to dark bread made from a special wheat. He sprinkles the whole thing with gold dust, a touch that is open to interpretation.

1   Preheat the oven to 340°F / 170°C.

2   **Make the lamb pâté:** In a large sauté pan, heat the butter over medium heat. Add the thyme, sage, rosemary, and marjoram. Add the lamb meat and brown on all sides, about 5 minutes. Add the lamb liver and brown on all sides, about 4 minutes. Pour in the red wine. Continue to cook until the wine has reduced by half. Discard the herbs. Remove from the heat and let cool.

3   Season the meat mixture with the vinegar, salt, and *colatura*. Transfer the meat mixture to a food processor and pulse until you get a smooth pâté, adding a few teaspoons of water if the mixture is on the dry side.

4   **To serve:** Spread the pâté on the pieces of bread. Place each piece in a shallow bowl and spoon the lamb reduction on top, adding enough so that the bread soaks up as much stock as possible. Add a spoonful of Montepulciano wine and, if desired, sprinkle the gold powder on top.

NOTE: *The idea is to use the crusty part of the bread, because it looks most like a piece of meat. When Niko Romito makes this, he uses a dark bread made with Solina wheat. Solina is grown in and around Abruzzo's Gran Sasso mountains, particularly the inland areas on the L'Aquila side, where the cold temperatures and high altitudes produce a grain of excellent quality. Just dip some bread in the leftovers of whatever one has just finished eating.*

# Lamb Reduction
*Makes about 1 cup / 250 ml*

2 TABLESPOONS EXTRA-VIRGIN OLIVE OIL

2 POUNDS / 900 G LAMB SHANKS

FINE SEA SALT

2 CELERY STALKS, FINELY CHOPPED

2 CARROTS, FINELY CHOPPED

2 ONIONS, FINELY CHOPPED

1 SPRIG OF FRESH THYME

1 SPRIG OF FRESH SAGE

1 SPRIG OF FRESH ROSEMARY

1 SPRIG OF FRESH MARJORAM

¼ CUP / 60 ML DRY WHITE WINE

¼ CUP / 60 ML SWEET RED WINE

*SERVING*

4 PIECES
(3½ OUNCES / 100 G
EACH) SOURDOUGH
OR RUSTIC COUNTRY
BREAD, PREFERABLY
THE CRUSTY PARTS
OF THE BREAD
ONLY (SEE NOTE),
TOASTED

LAMB REDUCTION
(RECIPE AT LEFT)

SEVERAL SPOONFULS
OF MONTEPULCIANO
DI ABRUZZO

1 TEASPOON EDIBLE
GOLD DUST POWDER
(OPTIONAL)

In a large pot, heat the olive oil over medium heat. Brown the lamb shanks on all sides. Season with salt and add the celery, carrots, onions, thyme, sage, rosemary, and marjoram. Pour in the wines and cover with 1½ quarts / liters water. Reduce the heat to low and cook, uncovered, until the stock is reduced to 1 cup of thickened and intense reduction, about 5 hours. Strain and season with salt.

PASTA

# *PRIMI*

hat I'm about to write now is probably controversial. There is so much to Italian cooking, including a rich history of beautiful fish and meat. But this is the chapter that means the most. The part of the story the world expects, where you make or break a meal. Part one, antipasti, is about ingredients. Source the best dried sausage, pair it with a great wine, and you pass with honors. For *primi*, however, there is no hiding. You must deliver. The pasta must be cooked to perfection. Everybody you'll ever invite has had it all before, and there is no margin for error in the execution. One of my favorite pastas is spaghetti with olive oil and chiles. Only that. Like bread and butter. But with bread, you can blame your baker; it's out of your hands. With pasta, it's all you. You take the glory and the shame. I have never, and will never, make pasta without a hint of fear and excitement. In no other cooking technique is the line between acceptable and transcendent so sharp. Pasta is rarely awful. (Well, it can be, but let's assume we're past that stage.) Truly great, though, is hard to achieve. A perfectly cooked pasta, from the best pasta maker, in a sauce that's simple and thoughtful and precise, that coats every string but doesn't overdo it. It's as elusive as anything. There are a few tricks. Undercook the pasta, always. Keep some of the cooking water. Finish in a big, broad pan where every piece has space where it can dance with the sauce. Glaze it, care for it, remembering that every bite should be special. Arrange the pieces on the plate as you would pieces in a puzzle. Do it fast. Risotto is the same: You are already happy, that prosciutto was satisfying. Now, there is a small amount of rice in front of you, some wine to go with it. It's not a filler, it's a delight. A few forks of pleasure. You can't really describe it. No other cuisine has this bridge between where you start and where you go. Other food cultures have comparable starters and meat dishes, but the bridge makes the difference. It's Italian.

THERE ARE STRIKING SIMILARITIES BETWEEN THE AMALFI COAST and the Ligurian coast. Incredible villages set against the backdrop of austere cliffs, the bluest ocean you'll ever find. Vespas driving perilously close to the rocks or the water. Reckless divers, tan and shiny swimmers. Glorious seafood, fritto misto. The key difference between the two coasts is in the color of the pasta sauce. Swapping red for green is swapping Positano for Portofino. Liguria is all about pesto, the thick, delicious green sauce that everybody loves, even children who don't eat vegetables. Ligurian basil is of incredible quality and grown in such abundance in the hills above the Ligurian sea. The other acclaimed Ligurian food is focaccia; made in some version all over Italy, the strongest traditions are here, where the local version is salty, oily, moist, crunchy, sometimes flavored with herbs. Often the best breakfast you can have is the simplest: a freshly baked focaccia and an espresso, early in the morning. With a view of the sea, of course.

We had never really stayed in Liguria, at least not on land. Passing by on our way from France to somewhere else in Italy, stopping for a beautiful, candlelit dinner in a seaside village before moving on the following day. In recent years, we've been to Portofino quite often, but it seems most of our time has been spent at sea. That's how I've been happiest in Liguria, in the water or on the water. A quick lunch, a rented boat, then a whole afternoon happily marooned with the family, somewhere between Santa Margherita and Portofino. Hours doing nothing but taking in the sun, reading, rolling into the ocean to cool off whenever needed. The older kids swim ashore in search of refreshments or adventure, sometimes bringing back wet focaccias that are surprisingly delicious when there is nothing else to eat. Once, friends generously lent us their boat for a few days, crew and all, which was the same thing but with a bigger boat and dry focaccia. We sailed along the Ligurian coastline, which stretches from the South of France to Tuscany. So narrow it feels like a piping on the coat of Piemonte. We visited the famous five villages of the Cinque Terre, which is a mistake in August: too many people, not enough space, though I imagine the same visit is gorgeous in late autumn. I remember us getting a fine in one of the villages, can't remember why though. We kept getting fines for the same things but never learned. Either it was some of our dogs doing something, or we brought a boat into the harbor, which wasn't allowed, or one of the kids did the wrong thing to the wrong person. In any case, the policeman was dressed like a general, though everybody else was almost naked. He screamed a little but changed his tone as soon as we accepted his fine. I don't remember us getting a receipt though.

We ended up in La Spezia and took the train back to Genova, a town that still remains a mystery to me. I guess my knowledge of eastern Liguria was very much restricted to Portofino and the surrounding villages like Camogli and Santa Margherita. Such a gorgeous part of the world, like a movie set, especially Portofino. In summer, you can't even go there—crowded, no parking to be had. As you drive along the coastline, suddenly you're stopped by police officers, almost always women, who tell you to go back and take a boat. Unless you have a hotel reservation. And of course you say you have one. Even if you don't.

As a result of our repeated and isolated marooning in Portofino, we had no particular friends in Liguria. We'd met some very good people, some restaurateurs with excellent food. I toyed with the idea of borrowing a pesto recipe as it felt appropriate and original. But in truth, I love my own. It's taken years to perfect. So I decided to share that one instead. This summer, however, we brushed up on our Ligurian knowledge and spent most of our holidays in the region, this time west of Genova, where we found far fewer international tourists but all the more Italians instead. Our days were curiously similar. We had rented a beautiful house in the Aquila valley just above Finale Ligure, sleeping with open windows so that when we awoke we had a slightly new rendering of the masterpiece that was our view. Every day we went to Varigotti, a slightly posh but very understated seaside town where the same Italian families have been coming for their entire lives. We bathed on the same beach, Bagni la Giara, and had lunch there every other day. We changed, slightly, what we ate, but there were staples we couldn't live without: The focaccia with anchovies and butter. The turkey sandwich with tuna sauce. Most of all, we always had the melon salad with ricotta, pine nuts, and arugula.

# CORZETTI
## WITH PESTO ALLA GENOVESE

*Serves 4*

2 GARLIC CLOVES, HALVED

FINE SEA SALT

2 TABLESPOONS PINE NUTS

3 BUNCHES FRESH BASIL, LEAVES PICKED, RINSED, AND PATTED DRY

6 TABLESPOONS GRATED PARMIGIANO-REGGIANO CHEESE

2 TABLESPOONS GRATED PECORINO ROMANO CHEESE

½ CUP / 120 ML EXTRA-VIRGIN OLIVE OIL

CORZETTI (RECIPE FOLLOWS), OR 1 POUND / 500 G STORE-BOUGHT DRIED PASTA OF YOUR CHOICE

esto needs no introduction: We all love it, the kids love it, and I'm sure you love it, too. If you have decent ingredients, it's very hard to get wrong. Cheating with a food processor is fine, but the purist, "correct," way to make it is with a mortar and pestle. For me, it's very simple. When I have time, I am all purist, and when I don't? I go electric. But don't tell anyone. And while I discovered my ideal ratio with pesto a long time ago, I've found that the quality of pesto depends largely on the quality of the basil, and I like to use a ridiculous abundance of fresh basil for my sauce. So the pestos I've made in Italy are probably the best I've ever made.

Pesto is often served with *trofie*, a small, twisted pasta native to Liguria. While I like to use *trofie* or even penne, my favorite way to serve pesto is with freshly made *corzetti*, an ancient medallion- or coin-shaped pasta embossed with a design. It's a ceremonial pasta, often reserved for the weddings of privileged families and stamped with the family crest using a wooden tool. The pattern can be anything: a beautiful illustration of a flower or whatever strikes your fancy. Pasta making is like anything else you get into, and the more you get into it, the fancier the tools you want.

1   Using a mortar and pestle, start crushing the garlic with ½ teaspoon of salt. When the garlic and salt have reached a creamy texture, add the pine nuts. Continue to crush. When creamy, add the basil leaves and continue the procedure, crushing in a circular motion. When all the ingredients are smooth, add both cheeses, then the olive oil, little by little. Continue crushing until all the ingredients are soft and creamy. Set the pesto sauce aside.

2   Bring a large pot of salted water to a boil over medium-high heat. Add the corzetti and cook until al dente, 3 to 4 minutes. Reserving a ladle of pasta water, drain the pasta.

3   Heat the pesto sauce in a large sauté pan over medium heat. Add the reserved pasta cooking water and let simmer until the sauce thickens. Add the drained corzetti to the sauce, tossing gently. Serve immediately.

## Corzetti
*Serves 4*

¾ CUP PLUS 2 TABLESPOONS /
100 G TIPO "00" FLOUR

¾ CUP PLUS 2 TABLESPOONS /
100 G SEMOLINA FLOUR

¾ CUP PLUS 2 TABLESPOONS /
100 G RICE FLOUR, PLUS MORE FOR
DUSTING (SEE NOTE ON PAGE 115)

2 LARGE EGGS

7 TABLESPOONS /
100 ML DRY WHITE WINE

PINCH OF FINE SEA SALT

1 In a large bowl, whisk together the "00," semolina, and rice flours. Mound the combined flour in the center of a work surface. Make a well in the center and add the eggs, wine, and salt. Using a fork, beat the eggs, wine, and salt together. Slowly incorporate the flour, starting with the inner sides of the well.

2 When the dough begins to come together, start kneading using the palms of your hands in a back and forth motion. Use a dough scraper to scrape away any stray bits around the pasta dough to tidy your work surface, as dried-out dough will interfere with your pasta making. The dough is ready when it is elastic and the surface gently "comes back to you" when pressed, 15 to 30 minutes. Wrap the dough in plastic wrap and let it rest for 30 minutes at room temperature.

3 When ready to roll out the dough, dust a work surface and rolling pin lightly with rice flour. Cut off a piece of dough (the equivalent of a handful), press with the palm of your hand onto the work surface, and roll out with the rolling pin to ½ inch / 1.25 cm thick. Set a pasta machine to its thickest setting and roll the pasta dough through it. Switch the pasta machine to the next thinnest setting and roll the pasta dough through again. Continue switching the settings lower and lower, until you get a thin and perfectly smooth sheet of pasta. Repeat with the remaining dough.

4 Dust a baking sheet with rice flour. Place a pasta sheet on a floured work surface. Use a *corzetti* stamp to cut the pasta shapes. Transfer the pasta to the prepared baking sheet. At this stage, the pasta can be covered with plastic wrap and stored in the fridge for up to 24 hours. You can also freeze individual portions for up to 3 months, making sure they are well wrapped.

# BASIC EGG PASTA

*Serves 4*

3⅓ CUPS / 400 G
TIPO "00" FLOUR

4 LARGE EGGS, AT
ROOM TEMPERATURE

RICE FLOUR (SEE
NOTE), FOR DUSTING

When I discuss making fresh pasta with my friends, many of them will say the same thing: They never, or hardly ever, make it because it's "so time-consuming and complicated." While I agree that you need to invest a bit of your time, I would argue it's time well spent. As for the complicated part, that's simply not true. Perhaps it seems complicated, but once you get the hang of it, the rest is easy. I love making fresh pasta as I find it therapeutic and stress-relieving to be in my kitchen, kneading and caressing, laying out the pasta sheets, cutting and shaping them into little gems. I take my time, listen to music, make sure I enjoy myself. It can also be very social: Invite people over early for a dinner party and have those who are game roll up their sleeves, often with a glass of wine nearby, and get to work. The joy is partially in the journey, though what a destination: a gorgeous plate of freshly made, perfectly cooked pasta, coated with a delicious sauce or stuffed with a beautiful filling—and the feeling of knowing that you made it yourself, from scratch.

1   Mound the "00" flour on a work surface. Make a well in the center of the flour and add the eggs. Using a fork, beat the eggs gently together. Slowly incorporate the flour, starting with the inner sides of the well.

2   When the dough begins to come together, start kneading using just the palms of your hands with a back and forth motion (the joke is that you should always be able to answer the phone while making pasta!). Use a dough scraper to scrape away any stray bits around the pasta dough, as dried-out dough will interfere with your pasta making. The dough is ready when it is elastic and the surface gently "comes back to you" when pressed, 15 to 30 minutes.

3   Place the dough in a large bowl and cover with a lid, a cotton cloth, or a plate. Set aside in the coolest part of your kitchen for 1 hour. (You can also prepare the dough the day before, wrap it in plastic wrap, and refrigerate. Before rolling, bring it back to room temperature.)

4  When ready to roll out the dough, dust a work surface and rolling pin lightly with rice flour. Cut off a piece of dough (the equivalent of a handful), press with the palm of your hand onto the work surface, and roll out with the rolling pin to about ½ inch / 1.25 cm thick. Set a pasta machine to its thickest setting and roll the pasta dough through it. Switch the pasta machine to the next thinnest setting and roll the pasta dough through again. Continue switching the settings lower and lower until you get a thin and perfectly smooth sheet of pasta. Repeat with the remaining dough.

5  Place the pasta sheet on the floured work surface. Cut and/or stuff the pasta according to your liking. The pasta will be fine at room temperature for up to 30 minutes, but if you're cooking later, cover the pasta with plastic wrap and refrigerate for up to 24 hours. You can also freeze individual portions for up to 3 months, making sure they are well wrapped.

NOTE: *Why rice flour? It's a light, gluten-free flour that's silky smooth; it won't thicken the water when you cook the pasta and will prevent sticking.*

# PUMPKIN RAVIOLI
## WITH BROWN BUTTER, CHESTNUT, AND SAGE

*Serves 6*

*FILLING*

1 SMALL PUMPKIN
(1 POUND / 450 G)

EXTRA-VIRGIN
OLIVE OIL

FINE SEA SALT

FEW SPRIGS OF FRESH
ROSEMARY

⅔ CUP / 60 G
GRATED PARMESAN
CHEESE, PLUS MORE
FOR SERVING

½ TEASPOON GRATED
NUTMEG

½ CUP / 75 G PLAIN
DRIED BREAD CRUMBS

FRESHLY GROUND
BLACK PEPPER

*PASTA*

1½ RECIPES (SEE
NOTE) BASIC EGG
PASTA (PAGE 114)

RICE FLOUR,
FOR DUSTING (SEE
NOTE ON PAGE 115)

his is my go-to winter pasta dish, the one I make almost once a week from November to February, and then never again until the next November. It's quite rich and filling, so I like to make fairly small portions, either for lunch or as the beginning of a comforting dinner when we all need a bit of color on our plate and some butter in our diet. The children love helping me—it's such an easy dish to make that, by the end of winter, they get so efficient they don't even need me in the kitchen.

1  **Make the filling:** Preheat the oven to 400°F / 200°C.

2  With a sharp chef's knife, cut the pumpkin into vertical slices 1 inch / 2.5 cm thick. Using a large metal spoon, scoop out the seeds and insides of the pumpkin and discard.

3  Arrange the pumpkin slices on a baking sheet. Drizzle with olive oil and rub on both sides of the pumpkin. Season all over with salt, toss with rosemary sprigs, and drizzle with more olive oil. Roast until fork-tender, about 20 minutes. When cool enough to handle, scoop the flesh of the pumpkin into a large bowl (discard the skins and rosemary sprigs).

4  Add the Parmesan, nutmeg, bread crumbs, and salt and pepper to taste. Stir well to combine. Set the filling aside

5  **Make the pasta:** Prepare as directed, divide into two pieces, and roll into two long sheets. Scatter rice flour over a work surface. Place the pasta sheets on the surface. On one sheet, carefully scoop 1 teaspoon filling every 3 to 4 inches / 8 to 10 cm. Drape the second sheet of pasta over the first one, gently pushing around each filling mound with your fingers to seal and remove any air bubbles. Trim each ravioli parcel with a sharp knife or a pasta stamp of your choice to form a neat shape, whether square, oval, or round.

6  Line a baking sheet with wax paper and scatter a good amount of rice flour on top. Transfer the ravioli to the baking sheet. Cover loosely with a kitchen towel and set aside in a cool place until ready to cook.

7   Bring a large pot of salted water to a boil over medium-high heat. Drop the ravioli into the boiling water and stir gently. Cook until they float to the surface, 1 to 2 minutes.

8   **Meanwhile, make the sauce:** In a 12- to 14-inch / 30 to 35 cm sauté pan, melt the butter over medium heat until it foams. Add the sage leaves and cook until crispy, about 1 minute. Add the chopped chestnuts and toss in the pan so they get coated with the butter. Add 2 tablespoons of the pasta water and shake the pan vigorously to thicken the sauce.

9   Scoop out the ravioli with a slotted spoon and transfer to the butter and sage. Toss gently over medium heat to coat the pasta with the sauce. Transfer to plates and grate Parmesan on top before serving.

NOTE: *To make 1½ times the basic pasta recipe, use 6⅔ cups / 600 g tipo "00" flour and 6 large eggs.*

*SAUCE*

10 TABLESPOONS /
150 G SALTED
BUTTER,
CUT INTO CUBES

15 FRESH SAGE
LEAVES

15 CHESTNUTS,
COOKED, PEELED,
AND COARSELY
CHOPPED

PRIMI

117

# *ANOLINI*
## *WITH RICOTTA AND HAZELNUTS*

*Serves 4*

*FILLING*

8 OUNCES / 230 G
RICOTTA DI BUFALA

½ CUP / 45 G
GRATED PARMESAN
CHEESE, PLUS MORE
FOR SERVING

2 OUNCES / 60 G
COARSELY GROUND
HAZELNUTS, SKIN-
ON, PLUS MORE
(OPTIONAL) FOR
SERVING

1 TABLESPOON PLAIN
DRIED BREAD CRUMBS

1½ TEASPOONS FINE
SEA SALT (SEE NOTE)

*PASTA*

SEMOLINA FLOUR,
FOR DUSTING

ESPRESSO PASTA
DOUGH (RECIPE
FOLLOWS)

*SAUCE*

10 TABLESPOONS /
150 G SALTED
BUTTER, CUT
INTO CUBES

15 FRESH SAGE
LEAVES

 laudia is the lady I call my pasta coach. She's incredibly passionate about pasta, the history, the old techniques. In other words, when it comes to pasta, she doesn't fool around. I love spending time with her, catching up, making pasta together. She's stronger than I am, a real *pastaio*, the person who makes pasta. It's encouraging to see young people like her, so committed to preserving the old traditions, thirsty for knowledge, and happy to share. These *anolini* are one of the recipes we've most enjoyed cooking together. It feels very exciting to add coffee to the dough, and the ricotta filling with the Piedmontese hazelnuts is heaven.

1   **Make the filling:** In a large bowl, combine the ricotta, Parmesan, ground hazelnuts, bread crumbs, and salt. Mix gently and set aside.

2   **Prepare the pasta:** Scatter semolina flour all over a work surface. Spread out a pasta sheet, then place small balls (about the size of a hazelnut) of the ricotta filling on one half of the pasta dough, about 1 inch / 2.5 cm apart.

3   Fold the sheet of pasta in half to cover the filling, gently pushing around each filling mound with your fingers to seal and remove any air bubbles. There should be no air in the *anolini*, otherwise they may open during cooking.

4   Cut the pasta using an *anolini* pasta stamp, so that in the center of each *anolino* there is just one ball of filling. Dust a large baking sheet with semolina flour. Transfer the *anolini* to the baking sheet and continue until you use up all the pasta dough.

5   Bring a large pot of salted water to a boil over medium-high heat. Drop the *anolini* into the boiling water and stir gently. Cook until they float on the surface, about 2 minutes

6   **Meanwhile, make the sauce:** In a 12- to 14-inch / 30 to 35 cm sauté pan, melt the butter over medium heat until it foams. Add the sage leaves and cook until the leaves are golden, about 4 minutes. Add 2 tablespoons of the pasta water and shake the pan vigorously to thicken the sauce.

7 Scoop out the *anolini* with a slotted spoon and transfer to the butter and sage pan over medium heat. Toss gently so the pasta gets coated with the sauce.

8 Transfer to serving plates and scatter Parmesan cheese and chopped hazelnuts (if using) on top.

NOTE: *It's important that the mixture be on the saltier side.*

## Espresso Pasta Dough
### *Serves 4*

1 TEASPOON / 7 G FINELY GROUND COFFEE
(WE USE COLOMBIAN COFFEE FOR ITS STRONG FLAVOR)

1⅔ CUPS / 200 G SEMOLINA FLOUR

RICE FLOUR, FOR DUSTING (SEE NOTE ON PAGE 115)

1 In a small bowl, stir together 6 tablespoons plus 1 teaspoon / 95 mL water and the coffee until dissolved. Mound the flour in the center of a work surface. Make a well in the center of the flour and add the coffee mixture. Using a fork, slowly incorporate the flour starting with the inner sides of the well.

2 Make the pasta as directed in steps 2 to 5 of Basic Egg Pasta (see page 114).

# SARDINIAN RAGÙ
## WITH SAFFRON TAGLIATELLE

*Serves 4 to 6*

2 TABLESPOONS /
30 G UNSALTED
BUTTER

2 TABLESPOONS
EXTRA-VIRGIN
OLIVE OIL

4 SHALLOTS, FINELY
CHOPPED

1 GARLIC CLOVE,
MINCED

1 CINNAMON STICK

1 POUND / 450 G
FENNEL SAUSAGE,
CASINGS REMOVED

8 OUNCES / 230 G
CANNED CHERRY
TOMATOES, DRAINED

1 TEASPOON SAFFRON
THREADS, SOAKED
IN 1 TABLESPOON
WARM WATER

FINE SEA SALT AND
FRESHLY GROUND
BLACK PEPPER

SAFFRON
TAGLIATELLE
(RECIPE FOLLOWS),
OR 1 POUND / 450 G
FRESH PASTA OF
YOUR CHOICE

I've come to the conclusion that I could write a whole book with a hundred ragùs and they would all be different and all delicious. But that's another book. A ragù Bolognese was always going to be included for obvious reasons, and for the longest time a Neapolitan ragù—which has more tomatoes and onions than a Bolognese ragù and uses a whole piece of meat rather than ground—was also in my lineup. That is until I started experimenting with this one. This ragù is made with fennel-flavored pork sausages, which I love on their own, and, like a Neapolitan ragù, it's heavy on tomatoes. One of the key differences here is the addition of cinnamon, which transforms the sauce. Last May, I made this ragù for my husband's birthday, along with saffron-flavored fresh pasta. Basically we made it with tagliatelle, but I have this wonderful pasta cutting tool that makes the edges look like jewelry.

1   In a large saucepan, heat the butter and olive oil over medium heat. Add the shallots and cook, stirring, until translucent, about 4 minutes. Add the garlic, cinnamon, and sausage meat and cook, breaking up the sausage with a wooden spoon, until the meat is browned, about 10 minutes. Add the cherry tomatoes and gently mash them up to make a sauce. Stir in the saffron threads and water, and season with salt and pepper. When the mixture comes to a simmer, reduce the heat to low. Cook, uncovered and stirring occasionally, until thickened, about 30 minutes. Set the ragù aside.

2   Bring a large pot of salted water to a boil over medium-high heat. Shake off any excess flour from the tagliatelle and add to the boiling water. Cook until al dente, 2 to 3 minutes. Reserving a ladle of the pasta water, drain the pasta.

3   Heat the pan with the ragù over medium-high heat. Add the reserved ladle of pasta water and the tagliatelle and gently stir.

4   To serve, twirl one serving of pasta inside of a soup ladle to get the perfect swirl, then gently place it onto a plate. Repeat with the remaining pasta.

# Saffron Tagliatelle

*Serves 4 to 6*

3⅓ CUPS / 400 G TIPO "00" FLOUR

4 LARGE EGGS

2 TEASPOONS SAFFRON THREADS,
SOAKED IN 1 TABLESPOON WARM WATER

½ TEASPOON GROUND SAFFRON POWDER
(SEE NOTE)

RICE FLOUR, FOR DUSTING
(SEE NOTE ON PAGE 115)

1 Mound the "00" flour on a work surface. Make a well in the center of the flour and add the eggs. Using a fork, beat the eggs gently together. Slowly incorporate the flour, starting with the inner sides of the well.

2 When the dough begins to come together, add the saffron water and powder and start kneading using the palms of your hands with a back and forth motion. Use a dough scraper to scrape off any stray bits around the pasta dough to tidy your work surface, as dried-out dough will interfere with your pasta making. The dough is ready when it is elastic and the surface gently "comes back to you" when pressed, 15 to 30 minutes.

3 Place the dough in a large bowl and cover with a lid, a cotton cloth, or a plate. Set aside in the coolest part of your kitchen for 1 hour. (You can also prepare the dough the day before, wrap in plastic wrap, and refrigerate. Before rolling, bring it back to room temperature.)

4 When ready to roll out the dough, dust a work surface and rolling pin lightly with rice flour. Cut off a piece of dough (the equivalent of a handful), press with the palm of your hand onto the work surface, and roll out with the rolling pin, about ½ inch / 1.25 cm thick. Set a pasta machine to its thickest setting and roll the pasta dough through it. Switch the pasta machine to the next thinnest setting and roll the pasta dough through again. Continue switching the settings lower and lower until you get a thin and perfectly smooth sheet of pasta. Repeat with the remaining dough.

5 Dust a baking sheet with rice flour. Place one of the pasta sheets on the work surface. Cut the sheet to your preferred length (16 to 20 inches / 40 to 50 cm is about right), then dust lightly with flour and pass through the pasta machine using the tagliatelle attachment. Place loosely gathered bundles of tagliatelle on the prepared baking sheet. Repeat the process for the remaining pasta dough. At this stage, the pasta can be covered with plastic wrap and stored in the fridge for up to 24 hours. You can also freeze individual portions for up to 3 months, making sure they are well wrapped.

NOTE: *We call for both saffron threads and powder because the powder helps provide that extra pop of vibrant yellow color to the dough. If you can't find powder, use a few extra threads.*

I REMEMBER READING ONCE THAT THE BEST PLACE TO EAT, ANY-
where in the world, is Bologna. Then I read it again somewhere else. I've been
to Bologna a few times since, and now that I am writing about Bologna myself,
I revisit these words and wonder if they're true, or at least true to me. I do
really like Bologna, a truly beautiful, prosperous city. A university city with an
international air. I like the style of it, the medieval feeling. It reminds me a bit
of Toulouse, another pink city. Food is certainly everywhere. Emilia-Romagna's
contribution to what is considered Italian cooking is undeniable, starting with
what the world often calls "spaghetti Bolognese." It's a dish that doesn't really
exist, seeing that in Bologna, the sauce is served with tagliatelle or another flat
pasta and is simply called *ragù*, a term used for meat sauce. Outside of the province, the sauce might be referred to as *ragù alla bolognese*. It's interesting when
a dish gets so famous that is ceases to be a recipe and becomes an idea, and a
vague one at that. These days, outside Italy, any pasta sauce made with ground
meat is called a Bolognese, although many of them are far simpler, made more
quickly, often with different ingredients, and sometimes closer to a Neapolitan
sauce due to a heavy use of tomatoes. The meat sauces in Emilia-Romagna
are quite dominant, but the region also touts vegetable-based varieties, such as
mushroom-based pasta sauces and raviolis (cappelletti) stuffed with ricotta or
pumpkin. Tortellini, another famous export, are admittedly stuffed with meat,
but served either floating in chicken stock or with a heavy cream sauce.

Emilia-Romagna has also given the world Parmesan cheese (Parmigiano-
Reggiano); *lasagne al forno*; many quintessential Italian cold cuts (*salumi*),
including mortadella, pancetta, prosciutto from Parma, and culatello; and the
wonderful balsamic vinegar of Modena, which is sometimes used as a base
for a sauce served with beef. During the holidays, especially New Year's, all of
northern Italy seems to be eating *zampone,* which is from Modena as well. It's
a sausage of sorts, made by stuffing the skin and front part of a pig's trotter
with various cuts of pork. It's then boiled and served with lentils. It's a dish
that grows on you, and I'm sure that if I live in Italy long enough, I won't be
able to imagine the festivities without it, but I'm not there yet.

Emilia-Romagna cuts through the Italian peninsula, from west to east, almost
from coast to coast. As you drive through, the richness of the land is obvious:

From Piacenza to Parma, Modena and Bologna, everywhere you pass is the home of some dish or produce you've been eating all your life. A sizable part of the region includes the coastal areas, the Adriatic beaches, which feel almost out of character or "off-brand" for a region mainly associated with meat and cheese.

This being a cookbook rather than a travel guide, I think the most important question about Emilia-Romagna is the one I asked at the beginning: Is it really the best place in the world to eat? Probably not, if you're a vegetarian. We play these food games at our house and with friends. Questions like "Which five ingredients would you take to a desert island?" "What would be your last meal?" You would be surprised how many people choose ragù. Or maybe it isn't surprising at all. In my favorite food movie, *Big Night,* the master chef telling a friend about lasagne with ragù says, "It's so good, after you eat it, you can't live, you have to kill yourself." I have always loved ragù, and it was my father's favorite Western food. But I have never wanted to kill myself over it and have been haunted by these words. For years, we've had this idea to find the place in Bologna where you can have the best ragù in the world, so that we, too, would want to kill ourselves. We found some great ones, especially outside of Bologna, but not necessarily better than the best we'd had elsewhere. The ultimate ragù still remains elusive, which is fine, as the pleasure is in the journey.

No doubt the standard of eating is high in Emilia-Romagna. But like anywhere else in the world, there's a huge difference between good and great, even in Bologna. To find the great, you have to look, put in the work, be a little lucky, have good tips. Food shopping, however, might be the best in the world: I sometimes go to Bologna just to get lost in the endless traditional food stores, losing myself among the stacks of Parmesan cheese, hypnotized by the countless hams hanging from the rafters of every store. We drove all over Italy in making this book, and we always stopped in Bologna on our way home to bring back incredible goodies for those of the family not traveling with us. I guess that's what Bologna is to me: a moveable feast, a literal one, just like the ragù itself.

Food shopping aside, my favorite activity in Emilia-Romagna is just driving in the countryside, trying to find the best places to eat. That's how we found our good Italians in the region. Two families running two incredible restaurants, and sharing their recipes on pages 128 and 134.

# TORTELLINI IN BRODO
## FROM MIRASOLE

*Serves 4*

2 TABLESPOONS
EXTRA-VIRGIN OLIVE
OIL

¼ POUND / 110 G
PORK LOIN

1 SPRIG OF FRESH
ROSEMARY

1¾ OUNCES / 50 G
MORTADELLA

1¾ OUNCES / 50 G
PROSCIUTTO DI
PARMA

½ CUP / 45 G GRATED
PARMIGIANO-
REGGIANO CHEESE,
PLUS MORE FOR
SERVING

1 LARGE EGG

1 TEASPOON FINE
SEA SALT

½ TEASPOON GRATED
NUTMEG

RICE FLOUR,
FOR DUSTING (SEE
NOTE ON PAGE 115)

BASIC EGG PASTA
(PAGE 114)

CAPON AND BEEF
STOCK (RECIPE
FOLLOWS)

I have nothing but admiration for *tortellini in brodo*. Elsewhere in this book, I talk about how we take ravioli and tortellini dishes for granted, as they exist in so many watered-down versions that many people have forgotten how noble they are—and you can see just how beautiful they *look* on page 125. Ravioli were once only made for special occasions, such as weddings, religious celebrations, and birthdays. Making tortellini for twenty people or forty or one hundred is no small undertaking. Stuffing them with the finest ingredients available, then boiling them in the heavenly broth of a fat capon as we do here, I can imagine the ceremony, the sense of exclusivity when the guests were seated at long tables and finally brought the spoons to their mouths.

There are various ways to make good tortellini, and while I have made many good ones myself, I have so much respect for this dish that I wanted to find an original version to include in this book. After a long search, this is the one I like best. I found it in Emilia-Romagna, of course, in a little family trattoria called Antica Osteria del Mirasole. The tortellini are very classic, but the broth is a little more elaborate than most versions with its inclusion of beef. Now we try to go to Mirasole whenever we are passing through Emilia-Romagna, and the headache is deciding whether to order the tortellini in cream or in broth.

1 In a sauté pan, heat the olive oil over medium heat. Add the pork loin and rosemary and brown the pork on all sides. Remove from the pan and let cool.

2 Cut the pork into chunks and place in a food processor. Pulse until finely minced, then add the mortadella and prosciutto and pulse until a paste forms. (Alternatively, use a meat grinder attachment. You'll want the mixture finely minced; if necessary, grind the meat twice.) Add the Parmigiano-Reggiano, egg, salt, and nutmeg and pulse until combined. Transfer to a large bowl, cover, and refrigerate until chilled.

3   Dust a work surface with rice flour. Lay the pasta sheets out on the floured surface and cut into 1½- to 2-inch / 3 to 4 cm squares. Dust a baking sheet with rice flour.

4   Remove the filling from the refrigerator. Shape ½-teaspoon amounts into small balls and place them in the center of each square of pasta dough. Fold the dough in half to form a triangle over the filling, gently pushing around the filling with your fingers to seal and remove any air bubbles. There should be no air in the tortellini, otherwise they will break when boiled. Take a triangle of tortellini and gently press the filling upward, toward the fold, with your thumb. Bring the two ends together to meet and press them with your thumb to seal. Set on a baking sheet and repeat with the remaining pasta dough and filling.

5   In a large pot, bring the stock to a boil. Add the tortellini and cook until they rise to the surface, about 2 minutes. Ladle the tortellini and stock into bowls and serve immediately with grated Parmigiano-Reggiano.

## Capon and Beef Stock
*Makes about 10 cups / 2.4 liters*

¼ CAPON (2 POUNDS / 900 G), CUT INTO 4 PIECES

1 POUND / 500 G BEEF TENDERLOIN, CUT INTO 2 PIECES

10 OUNCES / 300 G BEEF SHOULDER, CUT INTO 2 PIECES

1 BEEF BONE (ABOUT 3.3 POUNDS/1.5 KG) (KNUCKLE OR SHORT RIB)

5 CELERY STALKS, COARSELY CHOPPED

3 CARROTS, COARSELY CHOPPED

2 YELLOW ONIONS, HALVED

1 TOMATO, HALVED

2 PARMIGIANO-REGGIANO CHEESE RINDS (ABOUT 3 INCHES)

2 TABLESPOONS COARSE SEA SALT

In a large pot, combine all the ingredients with 3 quarts / liters water. Cover and bring to a boil over high heat, then reduce to medium-low. Continue to cook, covered, for 3 hours, stirring from time to time. Strain the stock and discard the solids.

# TAJARIN
## WITH TOMATO AND BASIL SAUCE

*Serves 4*

5 TABLESPOONS
EXTRA-VIRGIN OLIVE
OIL

1 GARLIC CLOVE,
SMASHED AND
PEELED

16 OUNCES / 460 G
PEELED TOMATOES,
DRAINED

FINE SEA SALT

1 POUND / 500 G
FRESH TAJARIN, OR
12 OUNCES / 400 G
DRIED TAGLIOLINI

A LARGE BUNCH OF
FRESH BASIL,
LEAVES CHOPPED

 few years ago, Oddur was writing a story on Torino for *Condé Nast Traveler*. Al Gatto Nero was on his list as a place of interest; it was originally a Tuscan restaurant, but over time it had become a Piedmontese institution. When he went there to take photos, he asked the chef to cook something, anything, just so he could get some kitchen shots. The chef and Andrea (the owner) both thought this simple tomato pasta might do the trick. After the shoot, the *tajarin* sat there in a bowl, getting colder by the second. Andrea saw Oddur glancing toward the bowl and offered it to him to try. "It's the best tomato pasta I've ever had," Oddur said when we met that afternoon. "You have to come back tonight with me." And I did. And for lunch the next day as well.

What makes this pasta so incredibly good? It's hard to say, really. The generous pour of olive oil, the abundance of basil? *Tajarin*, the most typical Piedmontese pasta, is most often served with local sauces, like ragù or Castelmagno sauce, but rarely with a tomato and basil sauce. That's what makes Gatto Nero unique: They have things others don't. I think the genius lies in the pairing of an oily tomato sauce mixed with the noodle-like pasta that creates a harmony of textures and flavors. It's the simple things.

1 In a large saucepan, heat the olive oil over medium heat. Add the garlic and cook until lightly golden, about 3 minutes.

2 Crush the tomatoes with your hands as you add them to the saucepan. Stir well and add ½ cup / 120 ml water. Cook for 20 minutes to reduce. Season with salt.

3 Bring a large pot of salted water to a boil over medium-high heat. Add the *tajarin* to the boiling water and cook until al dente, about 2 minutes.

4 Meanwhile, return the tomato sauce to medium heat. Reserving a ladle of pasta water, drain the pasta and add it and the reserved pasta water to the sauce. Toss for 20 seconds until coated.

5 Add the chopped basil and serve immediately.

# PASTICCIO DI MACCHERONI
## FROM ZIBELLO
### Baked Pasta Pie with Chicken Giblet Ragù

*Serves 6*

**PIE DOUGH**

1 POUND / 450 G
ALL-PURPOSE FLOUR,
PLUS MORE FOR
ROLLING

1½ STICKS PLUS
1 TABLESPOON /
200 G COLD
UNSALTED BUTTER,
CUBED

5 TABLESPOONS /
62 G SUGAR

PINCH OF FINE
SEA SALT

4 LARGE EGG YOLKS

1 TEASPOON GRATED
LEMON ZEST

**RAGÙ**

3½ TABLESPOONS /
50 G UNSALTED
BUTTER

¼ CUP / 60 ML
EXTRA-VIRGIN
OLIVE OIL

1 ONION, THINLY
SLICED

½ CUP / 120 ML
CHICKEN STOCK,
PLUS MORE AS
NEEDED

PASTA

T rattoria la Buca di Zibello is the sort of restaurant we're always hunting for—authentic, old-fashioned, and beautiful. Zibello is a little village not far from Parma, and its claim to fame is its revered culatello, the finest form of Italian *salumi*—like prosciutto but made from the best part, the hind leg, or *culo*. Buca di Zibello makes their own culatello and serves it proudly as a delicious way to open the meal. What caught my eye on our first visit was the gorgeous pasticcio, the sort of food you read about in books but can rarely find in restaurants. To have this regularly, you need an Italian *nonna,* and I've never had one of those. Like most good trattorias, la Buca is a family affair, and they were happy to share the recipe with me—almost: always that Italian mix of wanting to share but also wanting to keep a secret. This is truly an incredible dish, genius even, taking an already delicious ragù and covering it in delight. One shouldn't have favorites, but I must confess, in this book, the pasticcio is one of mine.

1   **Make the pie dough:** In a large bowl, combine the flour, butter, sugar, and salt. Using only your fingertips, rub in the butter and sugar until the mixture is crumbly like sand. Hollow out a well, then add the yolks. Beat the eggs with a fork to blend them. Add the lemon zest and knead the dough enough so it holds together. Gather it into a ball, wrap, and refrigerate for at least 30 minutes to chill.

2   **Make the ragù:** In a medium pot or Dutch oven, heat the butter and olive oil over medium heat and stir until the butter is melted, about 3 minutes. Add the onion and sauté until softened, adding a few tablespoons of chicken stock to moisten. Add the chopped chicken giblets and season with salt and pepper. Add the white wine and Marsala wine and cook for 3 minutes. Add the tomato paste and the ½ cup / 120 ml stock. Cover and cook over very low heat until the sauce has thickened and is golden brown, adding 2 more tablespoons of stock if too dry, about 1 hour.

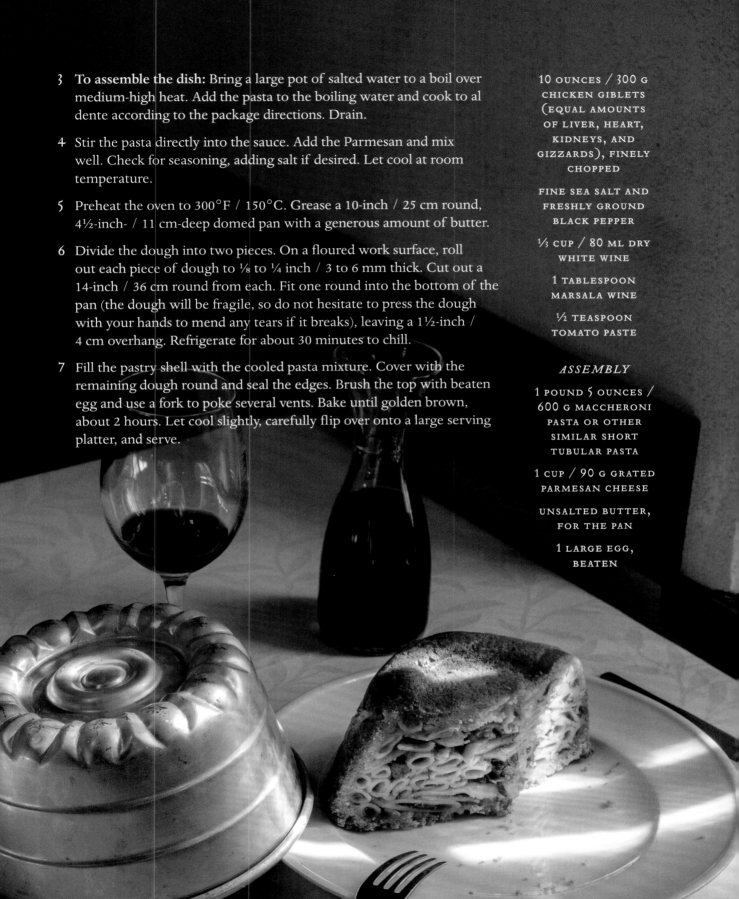

3  **To assemble the dish:** Bring a large pot of salted water to a boil over medium-high heat. Add the pasta to the boiling water and cook to al dente according to the package directions. Drain.

4  Stir the pasta directly into the sauce. Add the Parmesan and mix well. Check for seasoning, adding salt if desired. Let cool at room temperature.

5  Preheat the oven to 300°F / 150°C. Grease a 10-inch / 25 cm round, 4½-inch- / 11 cm-deep domed pan with a generous amount of butter.

6  Divide the dough into two pieces. On a floured work surface, roll out each piece of dough to ⅛ to ¼ inch / 3 to 6 mm thick. Cut out a 14-inch / 36 cm round from each. Fit one round into the bottom of the pan (the dough will be fragile, so do not hesitate to press the dough with your hands to mend any tears if it breaks), leaving a 1½-inch / 4 cm overhang. Refrigerate for about 30 minutes to chill.

7  Fill the pastry shell with the cooled pasta mixture. Cover with the remaining dough round and seal the edges. Brush the top with beaten egg and use a fork to poke several vents. Bake until golden brown, about 2 hours. Let cool slightly, carefully flip over onto a large serving platter, and serve.

10 OUNCES / 300 G
CHICKEN GIBLETS
(EQUAL AMOUNTS
OF LIVER, HEART,
KIDNEYS, AND
GIZZARDS), FINELY
CHOPPED

FINE SEA SALT AND
FRESHLY GROUND
BLACK PEPPER

⅓ CUP / 80 ML DRY
WHITE WINE

1 TABLESPOON
MARSALA WINE

½ TEASPOON
TOMATO PASTE

*ASSEMBLY*

1 POUND 5 OUNCES /
600 G MACCHERONI
PASTA OR OTHER
SIMILAR SHORT
TUBULAR PASTA

1 CUP / 90 G GRATED
PARMESAN CHEESE

UNSALTED BUTTER,
FOR THE PAN

1 LARGE EGG,
BEATEN

AS A LITTLE GIRL, I SPENT MANY SUMMERS IN SORRENTO. I WAS TOO young to remember much, but I recall standing on a cliff, my dress blowing in the wind, looking out at the ocean. The bluest in the world. I remember the intense beauty of the water, the bright red tomato sauces, balmy evenings, and the exciting pizzas. Mostly, I remember how elegant my mother looked every day.

Until I met my husband, I hadn't been back in over twenty years. Hours after we first met, he promised he'd take me to Ravello in the summer. At that point, I wasn't sure I'd let him take me anywhere. "It's the most beautiful place in the world, where the devil took Christ when he wanted to tempt him with earthly beauty," he declared. A few months later, I sat on a balcony in the hills of Ravello with breathtaking views and a Bellini in my hand. I had just found out I was pregnant and I had mixed feelings about it all. I was happy and afraid. Below in the garden, I saw Oddur, wearing a white linen shirt, striding across the garden, heading for the bar, probably to get another Bellini, although I can't remember. Was this the man I would spend the rest of my life with? Apparently he was.

We returned for three consecutive years. Each year, it seemed, with a new baby. We got to know the locals. We did the same things every day and every year. The annual trip to Capri. The day in Positano. Gelato in the evenings when everybody gathered in the piazza in front of the church. Each year, we walked down the steep hill to Minori where they have the best *delizia al limone* in the world, so good that even the Pope has made the trip. We fell in love with a little place called Cumpa' Cosima, but only ever called it "Mangia Mangia," because the old lady who owns it would tap our children gently on the head and say either that or *"Pasta, non pane."* They loved her and feared her in equal measure, which was also how they felt about their father. That last summer as we left, we promised to come back next year. But we went to Tuscany instead, then Marche, Umbria, and on, and have never returned.

Napoli has always been intriguing to me. The Amalfi Coast has all the glamour of a 1950s Technicolor movie: dark tanned men on flashy Vespas with flamboyant ladies riding behind them, hiding behind their sunglasses, smoking cigarettes, and dreaming of even richer, more tanned men who will take them to Capri. But Napoli, it always seemed to me, was the very heart of Italianata:

pizza, Sophia Loren, laundry blowing on balconies, men with slick hair in shiny suits, mozzarella, spaghetti alla puttanesca—a bustling, slightly dangerous but endlessly exciting city where high meets low. A city slathered in tomato sauce, with a gorgeous view of the sea. We had been before, but only briefly, for a pizza and maybe a coffee, usually on the way to the airport with no time to spare.

When I drafted my first shortlist of places to visit for this book, Napoli was number one. The city is so vibrant, so rich, always full of people—not as beautiful as Rome, but more exciting. So old-school, full of delicious pastries and pizza, dilapidated palazzos, men's tailors. Oddur jokes that it seems the city has only three types of stores: clothes for men, lingerie for women, and pizza for both. He isn't completely wrong.

There are, for obvious and historical reasons, many parallels between Neapolitan and Sicilian cooking. Both claim the famous Parmigiana. Tomatoes dominate the food scene. Delicious seafood and a plethora of local vegetables abound. Near Napoli is Gragnano, a small town between the Monti Lattari and the Amalfi Coast. It's the cradle of dried pasta and the reason why the people of Campania are the biggest consumers of pasta in the whole country. It's also where most of the best dried pasta in Italy still comes from. *Spaghetti alle vongole*, a "Best of" dish, is native to Napoli, as are the delicious sfogliatelle. Neapolitans also claim *babà al rum* as a local specialty, and while they make an excellent one, the French side of me is not quite ready to acknowledge that. In fact, the Polish side of me isn't either (my mother is French/Polish). The baba originated in Poland, was perfected in Paris, and that's that.

Our good Italian in Napoli is a concierge named Marco Giuliano—the best I've ever met. We had arrived by car from Sicily, via Messina, a day early and weren't sure where to stay. As Oddur drove, I searched for hotels, and we ended up at Grand Hotel Parker's, which had also been recommended by friends. The hotel was being renovated and the lobby was full of posters and office furniture for a panettone festival the following day. We got one of the unrenovated rooms with a strange layout and weren't even sure we were well located in the city. The following morning, Oddur went down to pay the bill and check out. Ever inquisitive, he had a good feeling about Marco, who was now on duty. Oddur asked for some recommendations and the answer he got lasted fifteen minutes. That morning, the lobby looked better, things had been arranged, so he extended our stay by three more nights, albeit in newly furnished rooms. "Whaaat?" was my reaction when he came back up and informed me. He told me about the concierge, the better rooms, and that we were actually pretty well located. I wasn't convinced. Going down in the elevator, I was joined by three heavily made-up young ladies in skirts so short that it seemed they only wore jackets. They were there to present panettone and someone must have thought this the perfect outfit rather than, say, a chef's hat. Only in Italy.

It turned out the panettone festival was incredible: Most people were dressed in normal length skirts and the panettones were some of the best I've ever had. Our two favorites came from Bergamo and Napoli. An organizer of the event was familiar with my books and asked me to pose for a picture. As I did, my cherished vintage sunglasses vanished. How Neapolitan is that?

Marco turned out to be a gem, his passion and knowledge completely infatuating. He was from the Spanish quarter, so a real Neapolitan through and through who knew everybody and was unfussy, charming, and passionate about food, and intensely passionate about pizza. He stood straight like a soldier, in the perfect uniform, with the broadest Italian smile and the softest voice. He completely understood what type of restaurants we like and rolled out a list of recommendations. His pizza recommendations were more like attending a lecture as he mentioned the best places, but also explained the differences. Pizza, we learned, is a Neapolitan art form. When he spoke about the Genovese sauce, it wasn't like a lecture, but a gospel, the most interesting sermon you'll ever hear. "This place makes a wonderful Genovese sauce, that one even better, but next time you come, give me some notice and I'll set you up for the best Genovese experience in the city—which means in the world," he told us. "I have this friend and he sometimes allows people to meet him in this basement where he cooks the sauce for thirty-six hours!" He then repeated with joyful seriousness, "Thirty-six hours."

When the concierge at your hotel changes your life for three days, you know he's the right man for the job.

# PIZZA MASTU GRAZIELLA
## Pizza with Tomatoes, Anchovies, and Lard

*Makes 4 pizzas*

DOUGH

1.7 CUPS /
400 ML
LUKEWARM
WATER (COLD IS
NEVER GOOD)

3½ TEASPOONS /
20 G FINE SEA
SALT

2 TEASPOONS/
8 G FRESH YEAST

5 CUPS / 600 G
TIPO "00" FLOUR
(OR A BLEND
OF "00" AND
"0" IN 60/40
PROPORTION),
PLUS MORE FOR
DUSTING

TOPPINGS

8 TEASPOONS
LARD, AT ROOM
TEMPERATURE

izza as we know it is originally from Napoli, and those who truly love pizza are convinced that Napoli is still where you can get the best in the world. Other regions have different styles—crunchier or pan-fried, different shapes, square rather than round—still, when it comes to pizza, Napoli lays down the law. I've tried many of the most celebrated pizzas in and around Napoli and many are truly fantastic, although I find a few a little sloppy and chewy for my taste. I wanted to include one pizza in this book, and while Napoli is where we started looking, Paris is where we ended up. Graziella Buontempo is a good-time girl from Napoli who moved to Paris for love (as one does) and opened a pizzeria (as one does if one is from Napoli). Her pizzas are as good as any I tried in Napoli, and since we lived for so long in Paris, I thought it would be fun to include her pizza in the book, and she happily agreed. So here it is (take a look on page 136). *Grazie,* Graziella.

Note from Graziella: The name and recipe derive from what is defined as the most ancient pizza recipe in Napoli (and sadly, practically impossible to find today), the Mastu Nicola, topped with only lard and Pecorino Romano. The Mastu Graziella is my personal take on this easy recipe, putting forward some of the best ingredients from the region.

1  **Make the dough:** Pour the water into a large bowl. Whisk in the salt until dissolved, then the yeast. Once the yeast is dissolved, add the flour, a little at a time. Knead the ingredients together by hand for about 5 minutes; the mixture will still be somewhat moist. Transfer the mixture to a stand mixer with a dough hook and mix on low speed for about 15 minutes, until you have a smooth mass (this will allow the flour to absorb all the moisture). Cover the dough and let rise for about 1 hour at room temperature, until doubled in size.

2   Divide the dough into 4 balls. Transfer to a baking sheet and cover for another 6 hours in a dry and warm place (the ideal temperature is 73° to 75°F / 23° to 25°C). After 2 hours, the dough will be doubled in size and ready to use.

3   Preheat the oven to 525°F / 270°C for at least 30 minutes.

4   Place the dough balls on a floured work surface. Working with one at a time and starting from the center and working toward the edge, press firmly with the palm of your hand to flatten into an 8-inch / 20 cm round. Lift the dough and rotate until you get a 10-inch / 25 cm round. Transfer to a large baking sheet.

5   Working with one at a time, scatter about 2 teaspoons of lard across each dough round, spreading it evenly with the back of a spoon and making sure to stay about ½ inch / 1.25 cm away from the edges. Toss a handful of tomatoes across the dough and sprinkle with ⅓ cup / 30 g Pecorino Romano.

6   Bake until golden brown and bubbling, 10 to 12 minutes. (In the oven, the lard will melt with the cheese and form a very flavorful, light cream.) Scatter 4 anchovies on top, garnish with a few fresh mint leaves, and drizzle very lightly with olive oil. Serve immediately.

7   Repeat with the remaining dough and toppings.

4 HANDFULS OF HALVED PIENNOLO TOMATOES OR CHERRY TOMATOES

1⅓ CUPS / 120 G GRATED PECORINO ROMANO CHEESE

16 MENAICA ANCHOVY FILLETS, OR OIL-PACKED

A FEW SPRIGS OF FRESH MINT, LEAVES PICKED

EXTRA-VIRGIN OLIVE OIL, FOR DRIZZLING

# ZITI ALLARDIATI
## Ziti with Lardo, Spring Onions, and Tomatoes

One more example of "simple is best" and "ingredients are king" is this traditional Neapolitan pasta that I am borrowing from Graziella, whose little pizzeria in Paris has the best pizza in France. She's from Napoli and her pizzas are as good as any from her hometown. She had agreed to share the recipe for one pizza (page 142), but happily threw this recipe in as a bonus. She's that sort of a girl. You can make this pasta with the ingredients available to you and it will be lovely. Or you can source the real thing and the result will blow you away. Ziti is traditionally found as a very long, tubular pasta form that is broken by hand. Breaking it down to the right size is strangely satisfying and gives the pasta an "artisanal" feel. Graziella adds *lardo*, cured pork fat used in Italian cooking, to lend richness to the dish. The tomatoes she uses are a specific variety, quite unlike any other. They are from Napoli, grown around Mount Vesuvius, and are called either the *pomodorini del Piennolo del Vesuvio* or simply Vesuvio cherry tomatoes. Usually hung in clusters (which can be quite decorative in a kitchen) and sweeter than other varieties, they can be stored for a long time due to their thick skins. The longer you store them, the more their aroma and flavor intensify as they dry out.

1   Bring a large pot of salted water to a boil over high heat.

2   In a large skillet, heat 2 tablespoons olive oil over medium-high heat. Add the *lardo*, spring onions, and tomatoes and cook until the onions are lightly golden, the *lardo* has started to melt, and the tomatoes have "popped." Remove from the heat.

3   Add the ziti to the boiling water and cook until al dente, 12 to 14 minutes. About 1 to 2 minutes before the pasta is ready, return the sauce to medium-low heat and pour a ladle of the pasta water into it. Drain the pasta and add to the skillet. Add the Pecorino Romano and Parmigiano-Reggiano and continue mixing well until the pasta "slurps" and is very lightly creamy. (The "slurping" sound means you've reached the ideal *mantecatura* stage, and the pasta is perfectly mixed.)

4   Scatter the basil leaves over the top and serve immediately.

*Serves 4 to 6*

EXTRA-VIRGIN
OLIVE OIL

7 OUNCES / 200 G
LARDO, CUT INTO
THIN SLICES

2 OR 3 SPRING
ONIONS OR LEEKS,
THINLY SLICED

4 OUNCES / 115 G
PIENNOLO TOMATOES
OR CHERRY
TOMATOES

1 POUND / 500 G ZITI
OR OTHER TUBULAR
PASTA, SUCH AS
PENNE OR RIGATONI

⅔ CUP / 60 G
GRATED PECORINO
ROMANO CHEESE

½ CUP /
60 G GRATED
PARMIGIANO-
REGGIANO CHEESE

A HANDFUL OF
CHOPPED FRESH
BASIL LEAVES

# *RAGÙ GENOVESE*

*Serves 4 to 6*

1 CUP / 250 ML
EXTRA-VIRGIN
OLIVE OIL, PLUS
MORE AS NEEDED

1 POUND 5 OUNCES /
600 G VEAL FILLET
(LEG PART) IN ONE
PIECE (THE MEAT
WILL FALL APART IN
THE END)

FINE SEA SALT AND
FRESHLY GROUND
BLACK PEPPER

1 POUND 10 OUNCES /
600 G NEAPOLITAN
GOLDEN ONIONS OR
YELLOW ONIONS,
FINELY CHOPPED

3 MEDIUM CARROTS,
FINELY CHOPPED

2 CELERY STALKS,
FINELY CHOPPED

5 OUNCES / 150 G
PIENNOLO TOMATOES
OR CHERRY
TOMATOES

1 CUP / 250 ML
RED WINE

1 BAY LEAF

1 SPRIG OF FRESH
ROSEMARY

1 POUND / 500 G
DRIED CANDELA
PASTA (SEE NOTE)

 his ragù is odd for so many reasons. Let's start with the name. Genovese. It strongly implies that it comes from Genova, just like Bolognese is from Bologna. But it does not come from there and is, in fact, one of the treasures of Neapolitan cooking. Another curiosity is that meat sauces are usually served quite sparely (or any pasta sauces for that matter), just enough to coat the pasta. In this case, chunks of meat are served with the pasta (although some of the meat is sometimes reserved for serving on its own). Finally, the most curious thing about this incredible ragù is simply that it's not famous, or even well known, outside Campania. Let alone outside Italy. I rarely meet people who have ever had it. Yet the ingredients are humble and easy to source and it's so delicious. That is the real mystery to me.

This version is borrowed from a wonderful restaurant in Napoli called Europeo di Mattozzi. It's an institution in the city—the waiters have been there forever and so has the chef. It's family-run, obviously, and on the walls are copper pots and souvenirs from decades of glamour and feasts. Luigia, the owner's daughter, is a force: She handles the staff like a rugby coach (a popular one) and the guests like a dream. On my last visit, she even made a special pizza in my name as a surprise, one with fresh zucchini flowers, provolone, and basil. (They have great pizzas at Mattozzi, which is almost unheard of in Napoli. Good pizza is usually found only in pizzerias, where only pizza is served. A restaurant with good pizza is an anomaly.) I've had several delicious versions of ragù Genovese, but I think it's safe to say that this is my favorite (roasting the ragù in the end is a great little trick). *Grazie*, Luigia.

1   In a large cast-iron pot, pour in the olive oil, then add the veal. Cook over medium-high heat, turning it occasionally, until browned all over. Season with salt and pepper. Add the onions and cook until the onions are browned and start to dry out, about 15 minutes. Add the carrots, celery, tomatoes, red wine, bay leaf, and rosemary. Continue to cook until the vegetables are softened, mashing the tomatoes gently

if necessary with a wooden spoon, about 5 minutes. Reduce the heat to the lowest setting, cover, and cook until the meat has completely softened and the sauce has thickened, about 3 hours, stirring and turning the meat over once every hour.

2   Preheat the oven to 330°F / 170°C.

3   Transfer the covered pot to the oven and bake until the sauce is thick and the meat is so tender you can mash it with a fork, about 3 hours. Adjust the seasoning if necessary.

4   Bring a large pot of salted water to a boil over medium-high heat. Add the pasta to the boiling water and cook to al dente according to the package directions. Drain the pasta, add to the sauce, and mix well. Serve hot.

NOTE: *The preferred pasta in Napoli is called* candela, *but you can also use another tubular pasta, such as ziti or mezzani.*

# RAGÙ BOLOGNESE
## WITH TAGLIATELLE

Spaghetti Bolognese, the most famous Italian dish in the world, doesn't really exist. Well, at least not in Bologna. The mayor of Bologna recently got so tired of this misunderstanding that he took to the media to put the spaghetti connection to rest, for in Bologna, ragù is served with tagliatelle, which, along with tortellini and lasagne, are the best-known pastas of Emilia-Romagna. Ragù (meat sauce) originally comes from Bologna and this is undisputed. There is even an official version of this most famous of sauces, but many cooks, even in the ragù's hometown, apply their own twist. I've put a lot of work and time into the research: I've tried countless wonderful versions, and all the really good ones are quite similar but with subtle differences. One chef includes liver in the sauce, which makes it more gamy; another uses a lot of liquid and reduces like crazy until he has the desired consistency. But the one I loved the most is very true to the original recipe. No particular tricks, just a respect for tradition, great ingredients, and thoughtful execution.

1   In a large pot, heat the olive oil over medium-high heat. Add the carrot, onion, celery, and oregano. Cook until slightly colored, about 5 minutes. Add the pork and cook until browned, then add the beef and cook until browned, about 8 minutes. Add the red wine and cook for 2 minutes to reduce.

2   Reduce the heat to medium and stir in the tomato passata and tomato paste. Add the beef stock and stir well until the tomato paste is incorporated. Season with salt and black pepper. Reduce the heat to as low as possible. Cover and cook, stirring occasionally, adding a few tablespoons of beef stock if the mixture looks a little dry, until you get a smooth and rich sauce, about 3 hours.

3   Bring a large pot of salted water to a boil over medium-high heat. Add the tagliatelle to the boiling water and cook to al dente according to the package directions. Drain the pasta, toss into the ragù sauce, and mix gently to combine. Serve immediately with grated Parmesan.

*Serves 4 to 6*

3 TABLESPOONS
EXTRA-VIRGIN
OLIVE OIL

1 LARGE CARROT,
FINELY CHOPPED

1 MEDIUM ONION,
FINELY CHOPPED

1 LARGE CELERY
STALK, FINELY
CHOPPED

1 TEASPOON OREGANO

½ POUND / 230 G
GROUND PORK
SHOULDER

10 OUNCES / 300 G
GROUND BEEF

⅔ CUP / 160 ML
RED WINE

2 CUPS / 500 ML
TOMATO PASSATA
(STRAINED PUREE OF
RAW TOMATOES)

4 TABLESPOONS
TOMATO PASTE

1 CUP / 250 ML
BEEF STOCK, PLUS
MORE IF NEEDED

FINE SEA SALT AND
FRESHLY GROUND
BLACK PEPPER

1 POUND / 500 G
TAGLIATELLE PASTA,
FRESH OR DRIED

GRATED PARMESAN
CHEESE, FOR
SERVING

PRIMI

# SPAGHETTI ALLA PUTTANESCA

*Serves 4 to 6*

8 OIL-PACKED
ANCHOVY FILLETS

2 TABLESPOONS
SALT-PACKED CAPERS,
RINSED

¼ CUP / 60 ML
EXTRA-VIRGIN OLIVE
OIL, PLUS MORE FOR
DRIZZLING

2 FRESH
PEPERONCINI OR
OTHER HOT PEPPERS,
THINLY SLICED

4 GARLIC CLOVES,
THINLY SLICED

1 CAN (16 OUNCES /
450 G) CRUSHED
TOMATOES

16 OIL-CURED BLACK
OLIVES, PITTED AND
COARSELY CHOPPED

1 TEASPOON DRIED
OREGANO

FINE SEA SALT AND
FRESHLY GROUND
BLACK PEPPER

1 POUND / 500 G
DRIED SPAGHETTI

CHOPPED FRESH
PARSLEY LEAVES, FOR
SERVING

As you can see, I included so many pasta recipes in this book (too many, perhaps) that toward the end of writing, I decided to cull a few. With great regret, puttanesca was on the endangered list, and I had decided to leave it out. Then it struck me that what's really wonderful about this Neapolitan sauce is that none of the ingredients need to be bought fresh. While a well-made puttanesca reeks of freshness, it can be made with ingredients exclusively from your pantry. Canned olives, capers, tomatoes, dried pasta. This is the sunshine dish to make when you are snowed in or when stores are closed.

1   Bring a large pot of salted water to a boil over medium-high heat.

2   Drain the anchovies, pat them dry with paper towels, and coarsely chop.

3   Rinse the capers under running water, soak in fresh water for 10 minutes, then squeeze and drain.

4   In a large sauté pan, heat the olive oil over medium-high heat. Add the anchovies, peperoncini, and garlic and cook until the anchovies start to sizzle (you can hear a crackling sound) and the garlic is lightly golden. Add the capers, tomatoes, olives, and oregano. Increase the heat to high and cook until the sauce starts to bubble and thicken, about 5 minutes. Season with salt and black pepper. Set aside.

5   Add the spaghetti to the boiling water and cook to al dente according to the package directions. Reserving ½ cup / 120 ml of the pasta water, drain the pasta.

6   Heat the sauce over high heat. Add the pasta and some of the reserved pasta water. Toss the pasta until it's coated, adding more pasta water to loosen the sauce if needed. Serve immediately with a drizzle of olive oil and some parsley on top.

# SPAGHETTI ALLE VONGOLE

**S**paghetti alle vongole is a happy dish. I don't think I have ever eaten it and been unhappy. When I have it, all I can see are blue skies and blue sea. Sometimes I've had *vongole* with blue skies and blue sea in my actual view, but even when I'm looking at a wall in my home or a restaurant, it's still blue sea that I see.

Some people are intimidated by cooking with clams, which can take a while to soak and scrub. But once you're past that, I would argue that this spaghetti is one of the easiest dishes in the book.

1   Fill a large bowl or pot with salted water and add the clams. Let stand for at least 1 hour to eliminate the sand. Drain the clams and rinse several times until there is no more sand. Scrub if necessary.

2   Bring a large pot of salted water to a boil over medium-high heat.

3   In a large sauté pan, heat 4 tablespoons of the olive oil over medium-high heat. Add the clams, 2 of the garlic cloves, the wine, and some pepper. Cover and cook until all the clams have opened, about 5 minutes. Do not overcook them or they will be chewy and lose their taste.

4   Remove from the heat and use a slotted spoon to transfer the clams from the pan to a large bowl. Strain the remaining cooking juices through a fine-mesh sieve into the bowl. Discard the garlic.

5   Meanwhile, add the spaghetti to the boiling water and cook to al dente according to the package directions. Drain.

6   Return the sauté pan to medium heat. Once it is dry, add the remaining 4 tablespoons olive oil and garlic clove. Cook for a few minutes until the garlic has browned, then discard the garlic. Add the tomatoes, clams, and half of the chopped parsley. Pour in the strained cooking juices.

7   Add the spaghetti to the pan and reduce the heat to low. Toss gently so the pasta is coated with the pan juices. Add a drizzle of olive oil, scatter the rest of the chopped parsley over the top, and serve immediately.

---

*Serves 4 to 6*

FINE SEA SALT

2¼ POUNDS / 1 KG CLAMS, SUCH AS LITTLENECK OR COCKLES

8 TABLESPOONS EXTRA-VIRGIN OLIVE OIL, PLUS MORE FOR DRIZZLING

3 GARLIC CLOVES, LIGHTLY SMASHED AND PEELED

⅔ CUP / 160 ML DRY WHITE WINE

FRESHLY GROUND BLACK PEPPER

1 POUND / 450 G DRIED SPAGHETTI

10 CHERRY TOMATOES, HALVED

A FEW SPRIGS OF FRESH PARSLEY, LEAVES PICKED AND CHOPPED

# CACIO E PEPE

Serves 4 to 6

2 TABLESPOONS
BLACK
PEPPERCORNS

1 POUND /
500 G DRIED
TONNARELLI OR
SPAGHETTONI
(THICK
SPAGHETTI)

3 CUPS / 270 G
FINELY GRATED
PECORINO
ROMANO CHEESE

NOTE: *To make this dish slightly easier to pull off (and maybe more delicious) but less authentic, heat 2 tablespoons / 30 g butter with the toasted peppercorns before adding the pasta water. This will emulsify the mixture better and create a richer (but greasier) sauce.*

When I was picking the recipes for this cookbook, the Roman pastas proved one of the biggest challenges. I was sure that I wanted to include at least one or two, but which? There are four pasta dishes found on the menus of many, if not most, restaurants in Rome. They are pretty much all the same recipe with one or two ingredients removed or added—a step-by-step thing. Cacio e Pepe, like the name suggests, has only cheese and pepper. Gricia adds guanciale. Carbonara goes a step further and famously includes eggs. Instead of eggs, Amatriciana has tomatoes. Cacio e Pepe would have been hard to leave out. The dish is simplicity itself, which can sometimes be the hardest thing to achieve—ingredients are key but the magic lies in the execution.

1   In a large, heavy skillet, toast the peppercorns over high heat until you hear a popping sound, 4 to 5 minutes. Remove from the pan and grind them with a mortar and pestle or spice grinder. Return the ground pepper to the skillet.

2   Meanwhile, bring a large pot of salted water to a boil over medium-high heat. Add the pasta to the boiling water and undercook by 5 minutes.

3   Reserving 1½ cups / 370 ml pasta water, drain the pasta. Add 1 cup / 250 ml of the reserved water to the pan with the pepper. Bring to a simmer over medium heat. Add the pasta to the skillet to finish cooking.

4   When the pasta is al dente, remove the pan from the heat and stir in the pecorino and remaining ½ cup / 120 ml pasta water. Quickly and vigorously toss the pasta with the sauce to make sure each strand of pasta is coated and the sauce is evenly emulsified. Serve immediately.

# PASTA ALLA GRICIA

**O**ut of all the Roman pastas, Gricia might be the one most often cooked in our house, as my husband frequently cooks it when we have little time and few ingredients. Well, that's how I wish it was. Like normal people. In reality, he likes to complicate things and serve Gricia before some other dish, which usually means late dinners and very full stomachs when going to bed. But his Gricia is delicious and had to be included. Simple preparation (the kids have gotten quite good at cubing guanciale and grating cheese), but timing and precision can be the difference between good and great. The good news is that while greatness is hard to achieve, Gricia, like Cacio e Pepe, is a satisfying dish even when made to slightly less than perfection.

*Serves 4 to 6*

10 OUNCES / 300 G GUANCIALE, CUBED

1 POUND / 500 G DRIED RIGATONI OR MACCHERONI

2¼ CUPS / 200 G FINELY GRATED PECORINO ROMANO CHEESE

1 TEASPOON COARSELY GROUND BLACK PEPPER

1   In a large skillet, fry the guanciale over medium-high heat, creating evenly golden brown, slightly crispy cubes, about 8 minutes. Remove from the heat. Let cool.

2   Meanwhile, bring a large pot of salted water to a boil over medium-high heat. Around the time when the guanciale is fried and starts to cool, add the pasta to the boiling water. Halfway through the pasta cooking time, add 1 cup / 250 ml of the cooking water to the guanciale in the skillet and set the skillet over high heat. Reduce the water by about half, or until it's reached a somewhat creamy consistency.

3   When the pasta is about 1 minute undercooked, use a slotted spoon (to avoid overdraining) to transfer it to the skillet with the guanciale. Toss well, adding more cooking water if the sauce gets too tight; it should have a slightly creamy consistency. Reduce the heat to medium, add one-third of the pecorino and all of the pepper, and stir well. Remove from the heat and stir in another one-third of the cheese.

4   Dish out and sprinkle the remaining cheese on the individual servings.

# SPAGHETTI ALLA CARBONARA

*Serves 4 to 6*

10 OUNCES /
300 G GUANCIALE,
CUT INTO ROUGH
½-INCH /
1.25 CM CUBES

1⅔ CUPS / 150 G
FINELY GRATED
PECORINO
ROMANO CHEESE

1 CUP / 90 G
FINELY GRATED
PARMIGIANO-
REGGIANO
CHEESE

2 LARGE EGGS

3 LARGE EGG
YOLKS

FRESHLY GROUND
BLACK PEPPER

1 POUND / 500 G
DRIED SPAGHETTI

If cacio e pepe and *gricia* are the boys who stayed home, carbonara is the brother who traveled the world, gaining incredible fame and popularity but losing something along the way, versions with cream or overcooked eggs, sometimes overcooked spaghetti. Bacon used in place of *guanciale* (pancetta) would be a better substitute. Not all terrible stuff, but very different from the boy who left home. I don't remember exactly when I had my first carbonara, probably not in Italy and certainly not at home. Most likely in an Italian restaurant in Hong Kong or Paris—I probably loved it even if it wasn't exactly the recipe that follows.

For magazine articles, people are sometimes asked to disclose what they always have in their fridge. Some of the answers are shocking to me (did you know that there are people out there with fridges that contain only Greek yogurt and bottled water?), because there are about a hundred things we always have. Included in that one hundred are the ingredients to make a proper carbonara. Always.

1  Bring a large pot of salted water to a boil over medium-high heat.

2  Meanwhile, in a skillet, fry the guanciale over medium-high heat to create evenly golden brown, slightly crispy cubes (never burnt on the outside and soft on the inside), about 8 minutes. Set aside.

3  In a large bowl, beat together the Pecorino Romano, ½ cup / 45 g of the Parmigiano-Reggiano, the whole eggs, egg yolks, and a generous amount of pepper. Add the guanciale to this mixture along with some of the fat, making sure it doesn't get too oily.

**4** Add the pasta to the boiling water and cook to al dente according to the package directions. Use tongs to transfer the pasta directly from the pot to the bowl with the egg and cheese mixture, tossing thoroughly so that each strand of pasta is well coated. Add a ladle of the pasta water directly from the pot to create a creamy texture. Serve immediately with the remaining ½ cup / 45 g Parmigiano on top.

# SPAGHETTONI
## WITH BAGNA CAUDA

*Serves 4 to 6*

3 RED BELL PEPPERS

2 TABLESPOONS
ANCHOVY CREAM
(RECIPE FOLLOWS)

1 POUND / 500 G
DRIED SPAGHETTONI
(THICK SPAGHETTI)

4 TABLESPOONS
EXTRA-VIRGIN
OLIVE OIL

1 CUP / 50 G FRESH
BREAD CRUMBS
(MADE FROM 3 SLICES
STALE BREAD WITH
CRUSTS ON)

A FEW SPRIGS OF
FRESH PARSLEY,
FINELY CHOPPED

FINE SEA SALT

4 TABLESPOONS /
60 G UNSALTED
BUTTER

1 GARLIC CLOVE,
FINELY CHOPPED

Luck was on our side the day we found our apartment in Torino. We chose it because it stands on a beautiful square, it has a terrace, and it suits us. What we didn't know was that the side street next to us is also the best street in Torino. It has some of our favorite stores and restaurants in the city, not least the wonderful Magazzino 52, a restaurant and wine shop where the menu is always small and market-based and the food is often the best you can find in all of Torino. Magazzino is run by three friends, two of whom are brothers. The Rista brothers, who come from Ivrea in northern Piemonte, worked for years in various prestigious kitchens and mastered the trade of classic Piedmontese cooking. Today, Dario, the younger of the brothers, helms the kitchen, and while his dishes are respectful of tradition, they feel like the perfect mix of modern meets classic: There is something so comforting and familiar about his cooking, but on the other hand, it also feels new. This is an interesting recipe that uses the flavors behind bagna cauda (see the recipe on page 71) as a base for a pasta sauce to wonderful effect. Dario recommends using spaghettoni, which is a thicker version of spaghetti, for the best results.

1  Preheat the oven to 480°F / 250°C.

2  Place the peppers on a baking sheet and roast, turning once, until they start to blister and blacken, about 25 minutes. Transfer to a medium bowl and cover with plastic wrap (this process makes peeling much easier). Let them steam for 10 minutes, then peel with your hands by stripping off the loose skin. Discard the stems and seeds. Slice the peppers lengthwise into fine strips, as thin as linguine. Set aside.

3  Make the anchovy cream and set aside.

4  Bring a large pot of salted water to a boil over medium-high heat. Add the pasta and cook to al dente according to the package directions. Reserving a ladleful of pasta water, drain the pasta.

5   Meanwhile, in a large sauté pan, heat 2 tablespoons of the olive oil over medium heat. Add the bread crumbs and parsley and sauté until golden and crispy, about 6 minutes. Transfer to a medium bowl and season with salt. Wipe out the pan.

6   In the same pan, heat the remaining 2 tablespoons olive oil over medium heat. Add the sliced peppers and lightly season with salt. Toss the peppers in the oil and cook until further softened, about 2 minutes. Remove from the pan and set aside.

7   Add the butter and garlic to the sauté pan and cook until the garlic is lightly golden, about 3 minutes. Add the drained pasta to the pan along with the anchovy cream and a ladle of pasta water. Toss to combine.

8   To serve, garnish the pasta with the strands of roasted peppers, then spoon the golden bread crumbs around the pasta.

## Anchovy Cream
### *Makes ¾ cup*

3½ OUNCES /
100 G OIL-PACKED
ANCHOVY FILLETS

3 TABLESPOONS
ICE-COLD WATER

2 TABLESPOONS
EXTRA-VIRGIN OLIVE
OIL

In a blender, puree the anchovies, ice water, and olive oil until you get a smooth cream. Store in an air-tight container in the refrigerator for up to 3 days. You can also use this cream as a dip or a sandwich spread.

# ORECCHIETTE
## WITH TENERUMI AND
## CHERRY TOMATOES

*Serves 4 to 6*

2 LARGE BUNCHES
(ABOUT 1½ POUNDS /
675 G) TENERUMI
(SEE NOTE)

1 POUND / 500 G
DRIED ORECCHIETTE

6 TABLESPOONS
EXTRA-VIRGIN OLIVE
OIL, PLUS MORE FOR
DRIZZLING

2 GARLIC CLOVES,
THINLY SLICED

1 TEASPOON CRUSHED
RED PEPPER FLAKES

FINE SEA SALT

10 OUNCES / 300 G
CHERRY TOMATOES,
HALVED

FRESHLY GROUND
BLACK PEPPER

¾ CUP / 65 G GRATED
PARMESAN CHEESE

NOTE: *Instead of*
tenerumi, *you can
use Savoy cabbage or
radicchio leaves.*

Having dabbled in gardening more than a little and being a firm believer in sustainability and organic farming, I am in love with the idea of finding new, delicious ways of eating sometimes overlooked produce. The organic farmers' market in Torino is one of the best in the world, and one day, in summer, I noticed everybody buying bundles of these wild, green, and very affordable leaves and shoots that looked like zucchini plants. I started talking with the locals, got inspired, and quickly hopped on the *tenerumi* train. *Tenerumi* are the leaves of squash plants and, to me, the equivalent of finding coins in your pocket, as cooking with them is tantamount to making something out of nothing, the treasure that was hiding before your eyes. We most often use *tenerumi* for pastas such as this one, where the slight bitterness of the greens marries spectacularly with the acidic sweetness of the cherry tomatoes.

1   Pluck the leaves off the stems of the *tenerumi* and discard the stems and any damaged leaves. Rinse and place in a salad spinner to spin dry. Cut the leaves into 1-inch / 2.5 cm strips.

2   Bring a large pot of salted water to a boil over medium-high heat. Add the orecchiette to the boiling water and cook to al dente according to the package directions. Reserving ½ cup / 120 ml of the pasta water, drain the pasta.

3   Meanwhile, in a large sauté pan, heat 3 tablespoons of the olive oil over medium heat. Add the garlic and cook until slightly golden, about 3 minutes. Add the pepper flakes. Increase the heat to high and add the cut *tenerumi* leaves. Continue to sauté, stirring occasionally, until tender, about 10 minutes. Season with salt. Add the remaining 3 tablespoons olive oil. Add the tomatoes and sauté for a few minutes to soften.

4   Add the pasta and reserved pasta water to the pan and mix everything together. Season with black pepper. Serve immediately with grated Parmesan and a drizzle of olive oil.

# SPAGHETTI
## WITH ZUCCHINI BLOSSOMS

Edible flowers come in and out of fashion, but zucchini blossoms have, unsurprisingly, long been a staple of Italian cooking. With their subtle, irresistible flavor, they are surely also one of the most beautiful ingredients imaginable. Strangely enough, in France, they are hard to come by, but here in Italy they flood the markets and local grocery stores. And I always fall for them, meaning I have to act fast as they wither quickly and demand immediate attention, which I am happy to give. This pasta is very easy to make and is excellent as a *primi* before a bit of meat or fish, but it also works very well on its own. All my vegetarian friends are fans.

*Serves 4 to 6*

25 ZUCCHINI
BLOSSOMS (ABOUT
4 OUNCES / 115 G)

1 POUND / 500 G
DRIED SPAGHETTI

6 TABLESPOONS
EXTRA-VIRGIN OLIVE
OIL, PLUS MORE FOR
DRIZZLING

3 GARLIC CLOVES,
2 THINLY SLICED AND
1 MINCED

2 CUPS / 100 G FRESH
BREAD CRUMBS

FINE SEA SALT AND
FRESHLY GROUND
BLACK PEPPER

1 TEASPOON CRUSHED
RED PEPPER FLAKES

¾ CUP / 65 G GRATED
PARMESAN CHEESE

8 SPRIGS OF FRESH
PARSLEY, LEAVES
PICKED AND CHOPPED

1   Remove the stamens from each zucchini blossom. Rinse and pat dry. Cut the blossoms into 1-inch / 2.5 cm strips. Set aside.

2   Bring a large pot of salted water to a boil over medium-high heat. Add the pasta to the boiling water and cook to al dente according to the package directions. Reserving ¾ cup / 180 ml of the water, drain the pasta.

3   In a large sauté pan, heat 2 tablespoons of the olive oil over medium-high heat. Add the minced garlic and bread crumbs and cook, stirring, until golden brown and crispy, 3 to 4 minutes. Remove the pan from the heat and add a dash of salt and pepper. Transfer to a bowl and wipe out the pan.

4   In the same pan, heat the remaining 4 tablespoons olive oil over medium-high heat. Add the sliced garlic and pepper flakes and sauté until the garlic is golden, about 2 minutes. Add the chopped blossoms and cook until tender, about 5 minutes. Season with salt and remove from the heat.

5   Add the pasta and ½ cup / 120 ml of the reserved pasta water to the zucchini blossom mixture. Toss to coat, adding more liquid if it seems dry. Stir in the Parmesan.

6   Serve topped with the garlicky bread crumbs, the parsley, and a drizzle of olive oil.

# CHICKPEA SOUP
## WITH MALTAGLIATI PASTA

This is another Italian dish that's open to interpretation rather than adhering to a strict dogma of how it must be. One of the most comforting foods I can imagine, so flavorful and filling, this recipe can be made with many different types of pasta; it can be creamy or clear, tomato-heavy or not so much. Of course, to live up to its name, there must always be pasta and chickpeas, but that's about it. In my version, I use *maltagliati* pasta (which means "badly cut") to give this rustic dish an informal flair. I love stock, so I make sure the result is more soupy than stewy, and I like to include some tomatoes for good acidity. Mostly, I ensure there is enough, because everyone wants at least two bowls.

1   In a large pot, heat the olive oil over medium heat. Add the garlic and rosemary and cook until fragrant, about 4 minutes. Add the chopped tomatoes and their juices. Cook, stirring occasionally, until starting to simmer, about 10 minutes. Stir in the stock and the chickpeas, reduce the heat to medium-low, and cook for 10 minutes.

2   Remove half of the chickpeas with a slotted spoon and add to a blender along with some of the broth from the pot. Blend until you get a smooth and creamy paste. Season with salt and pepper. Use a spatula to scrape the puree back into the pot. Stir to combine and let come to a simmer.

3   Add the pasta and cook until al dente, 6 to 8 minutes.

4   Serve with the chopped basil, a drizzle of olive oil, and a scattering of grated Parmesan.

*Serves 4*

3 TABLESPOONS EXTRA-VIRGIN OLIVE OIL, PLUS MORE FOR DRIZZLING

1 GARLIC CLOVE, PEELED AND SMASHED

4 SPRIGS OF FRESH ROSEMARY, LEAVES PICKED AND CHOPPED

1 CUP / 240 G CANNED CHOPPED TOMATOES, WITH THEIR JUICES

4 CUPS / 950 ML CHICKEN OR VEGETABLE STOCK (PAGE 33)

1 CAN (15 OUNCES / 425 G) CHICKPEAS, RINSED AND DRAINED

FINE SEA SALT AND FRESHLY GROUND BLACK PEPPER

5 OUNCES / 150 G DRIED MALTAGLIATI PASTA

A HANDFUL OF FRESH BASIL OR PARSLEY, LEAVES ROUGHLY CHOPPED, FOR GARNISH

GRATED PARMESAN CHEESE, FOR SERVING

PRIMI

# *BROCCOLI PASTA*

*Serves 4 to 6*

1 LARGE HEAD
BROCCOLI AND STEMS
(ABOUT 1 POUND /
450 G), CUT INTO
SMALL FLORETS AND
COARSELY CHOPPED

1 POUND / 500 G
DRIED SPAGHETTI

¼ CUP / 60 ML
EXTRA-VIRGIN
OLIVE OIL

1 ONION, FINELY
CHOPPED

1 GARLIC CLOVE,
MINCED

FINE SEA SALT AND
FRESHLY GROUND
BLACK PEPPER

½ CUP / 120 ML
HEAVY CREAM

1¼ CUPS / 115 G
GRATED PARMESAN
CHEESE

ike any good mother, I care what my children eat. I'm lucky I guess: They have grown up around so much food and cooking that very few things are alien to them. They've been eating it all forever, and there's never really been any need for manipulation. Still, there are the preferred foods and then there are a few villains. Broccoli is the benchmark; not that they particularly disliked it, but the inclusion of broccoli in a meal was rarely met with loud cheers. Sure, a broccoli gratin was well tolerated, and the roasted broccoli I often serve with salmon or Asian dishes was sort of liked. But none of it was ever beloved, until I struck gold with this pasta sauce. The first time I made it I must have been in a state of enlightenment, as I just thought of including broccoli in a creamy pasta sauce—frying it with onions to get the best flavors out of all the ingredients, creaming it up, adding Parmesan. One of my biggest hits to this day, I'm happy to say.

1  Bring a large pot of salted water to a boil over medium-high heat. Add the broccoli and cook until al dente, about 3 minutes. Remove with a slotted spoon and set aside, keeping the water boiling to cook the pasta.

2  Add the pasta to the boiling water and cook to al dente according to the package directions. Reserving 1 cup / 250 ml of the cooking water, drain the pasta, return to the empty pot, and set aside.

3  Meanwhile, in a large sauté pan, heat the olive oil over medium heat. Add the onion and sauté until tender and golden, about 5 minutes. Add the garlic and cook for another minute. Add the broccoli and season with salt and pepper. Pour the cream over the mixture. Cook for 15 seconds and remove from the heat.

4  Transfer the broccoli mixture to a food processor and process until roughly creamy.

5  Add the broccoli sauce and a few tablespoons of reserved pasta water to the pot of pasta and set the pot over medium-high heat. Cook, tossing frequently, until the pasta is well coated, 1 to 2 minutes. Season with salt and pepper and scatter the grated Parmesan on top. Serve immediately.

# SAGE AND WALNUT TAGLIATELLE

*Serves 4 to 6*

1 POUND / 500 G
DRIED TAGLIATELLE

12 TABLESPOONS /
180 G UNSALTED
BUTTER

FINE SEA SALT

20 FRESH SAGE
LEAVES, COARSELY
CHOPPED

⅔ CUP / 100 G
WALNUTS, LIGHTLY
TOASTED AND
COARSELY CHOPPED

¾ CUP / 65 G GRATED
PARMESAN CHEESE

FRESHLY GROUND
BLACK PEPPER

I can't remember how this pasta happened, but I do remember being in a hurry. I was probably going out with my husband, maybe to the opera or just on a date night. In France, it's very common to cook pasta shells with grated cheese and ham for kids, a kiddie meal that everyone likes. This was my elevated kiddie meal, just as simple but vegetarian, with two of my favorite healthy ingredients, walnuts and sage. It was a bit risky; maybe they wouldn't like it. Luckily they did, especially Gaia, who asks for this pasta every time she gets the chance to choose. Don't underestimate your children; they, too, know a delicious flavor when it hits their palate.

1  Bring a large pot of salted water to a boil over medium-high heat. Add the pasta to the boiling water and cook to al dente according to the package directions. Reserving a ladle of pasta water, drain the pasta.

2  Meanwhile, in a large saucepan (large enough to add all the pasta later), melt the butter with 1 teaspoon salt over medium-high heat. When it starts to simmer, reduce the heat to medium-low and let it cook until it starts to turn golden. Add the sage leaves and cook until golden, about 4 minutes. Remove from the heat and let the sage leaves continue to cook until slightly crispy. Add a pinch of salt. Set aside.

3  When the pasta is ready, heat the pan with the brown butter and sage leaves over medium heat. Stir in the walnuts. Toss in the pasta and the reserved pasta water and stir to combine. Sprinkle with the Parmesan. Season with salt and pepper and serve.

# GNOCCHI CASTELMAGNO

*Serves 4*

2¼ POUNDS / 1 KG
POTATOES, HALF RED
AND HALF YELLOW
VARIETIES

1 LARGE EGG

FINE SEA SALT

2½ CUPS / 300 G
ALL-PURPOSE FLOUR,
PLUS MORE FOR
DUSTING

¼ TEASPOON GRATED
NUTMEG

¾ CUP / 180 ML
HEAVY CREAM

FRESHLY GROUND
BLACK PEPPER

8 OUNCES / 230 G
CASTELMAGNO
CHEESE (OR
ANY STRONGLY
FLAVORED, CRUMBLY,
AGED COW'S MILK
CHEESE), CRUMBLED
WITH A FORK

Castelmagno cheese is the pride of Piedmontese cheeses, the "king of cheeses" as they call it locally. Unknown to me until I started spending time in Piemonte, it's an unusual cheese, crumbly but not dry, instead rather creamy, very flavorful, and even pungent and moldy when it ages past a certain point. The production is small and occurs only from April to October every year. It's a cow's milk cheese, though these are no regular cows, but ones that roam the steep hills of the Castelmagno valley. While I love it on its own with a glass of wine, it's really spectacular when melted into a pasta sauce, like a local version made for *tajarin* (tagliolini) with Castelmagno and hazelnut sauce. However, these gnocchi, which come from the mountains where they make the cheese, may be the best way there is to fully enjoy the cheese. The ladies who make them told me it's very important to include both red and yellow potatoes and to boil them with the skin on. So of course I do.

1   Place the potatoes in a large pot of salted water and set over medium-high heat. Bring to a boil and cook until the potatoes are very tender, about 40 minutes. Remove the potatoes with a slotted spoon and drain. Reserve the pot of water for cooking the gnocchi later.

2   Let the potatoes cool for 5 minutes, then peel. Place them in a ricer and rice the potatoes into a large bowl. Make a small well in the center of the potatoes. Add the egg and 1 teaspoon salt and beat the egg with a fork until smooth. Add the flour and nutmeg and mix slowly with a wooden spoon until you get a stiff dough.

3   Transfer the mixture to a floured work surface. Use your dough scraper to gather everything neatly. Knead the dough gently until smooth but slightly sticky.

4   Line a baking sheet with wax paper and dust with flour. Cut the dough into 4 pieces, then roll each into a rope ¾ inch / 2 cm thick, using more flour if needed. Cut the ropes into 1-inch / 2.5 cm pieces. Roll each piece against the tines of a fork to make ridges, then transfer to the baking sheet.

5   Return the reserved pot of water to a boil. Add the gnocchi and cook until they rise to the surface, about 1 minute.

6   Meanwhile, in a large nonstick skillet, heat the cream over medium heat. Using a slotted spoon, add the gnocchi from the pot to the cream. Season with salt and pepper and cook over high heat for 1 minute, until fully coated. Remove from the heat, sprinkle with the Castelmagno, and serve immediately.

NOTE: *The uncooked gnocchi pieces can be frozen on the prepared baking sheet, then transferred to a zip-seal freezer bag and frozen for up to 1 month. Boil without thawing.*

# GNOCCHETTI DI RICOTTA E SPINACI

*Ricotta and Spinach Gnocchetti*

*Serves 4*

1 POUND / 450 G
SPINACH LEAVES

16 OUNCES / 450 G
ITALIAN-STYLE
RICOTTA CHEESE OR
DRAINED REGULAR
RICOTTA

2 LARGE EGGS

½ TEASPOON GRATED
NUTMEG

FINE SEA SALT AND
FRESHLY GROUND
BLACK PEPPER

⅔ CUP / 80 G
ALL-PURPOSE FLOUR,
FOR DREDGING

5½ TABLESPOONS /
75 G SALTED BUTTER

15 FRESH SAGE
LEAVES

¾ CUP / 65 G GRATED
PARMESAN CHEESE

In 1973, Antonio Foscari, a professor and historian of architecture, and his wife, Barbara, bought back the villa that their family had lost during a period of financial difficulty centuries earlier. Villa Foscari, known as La Malcontenta, is no ordinary house. It is a Palladio masterpiece on the Riviera del Brenta, just outside Venice. The couple restored the villa lovingly to its former glory and did such a good job (she is also an architect) that it has been called "the most beautiful house in the world." I was intrigued to discover the house and pleasantly surprised to find out how committed the family is to serving great food. They've employed a cook since the beginning, each one putting in a shift of decades at the stove; their current cook, Rosanna, is the second holder of the job. The Foscaris even have a family cookbook, dedicated to the house, and they allowed me to pick my favorites from that very personal book to include in this one. One of the dishes that caught my eye were these spinach and ricotta balls called *gnocchetti*, a favorite of Antonio's son, Ferigo, who is now a grown man and a friend. The upper floors of the villa are sometimes open to the public, and while they are truly breathtaking, my favorite parts of the house are elsewhere, where I've spent time cooking with Rosanna, chatting with Antonio about food, and feasting in their private "simple" dining room downstairs next to the kitchen, the scene of the best action in any house, as we all know.

1   Bring a large pot of salted water to a boil over medium-high heat.

2   Add the spinach to the boiling water and cook, stirring occasionally, until just tender, about 2 minutes. Remove the spinach with a slotted spoon and drain in a fine-mesh sieve. Press the spinach with the spoon to squeeze out as much liquid as possible. This step is very important so the spinach doesn't release water. Reserve the pot of water for cooking the *gnochetti*.

3   In a large bowl, combine the spinach, ricotta, eggs, nutmeg, and salt and pepper to taste and mix with a wooden spoon until a slightly sticky dough forms.

4   Place the flour in a shallow bowl. Making one at a time, take a little dough (about the size of a walnut) in the palm of your hands, lightly dredging with flour to help shape each ball. Set aside.

5   In a small saucepan, heat the butter over medium heat. Add a pinch of salt and the sage leaves and cook until the butter turns golden brown and the sage leaves are crisp, about 5 minutes. Set aside.

6   Bring the reserved pot of water to a boil and add 1 teaspoon salt. Working in batches, add the *gnocchetti* to the water and cook until they rise to the surface, about 1 minute. Using a slotted spoon, remove the *gnocchetti* from the water and drain.

7   Place in a serving dish, drizzle with the sage-butter sauce, and sprinkle the Parmesan on top. Serve immediately.

IT'S A STRANGE THING, CONSIDERING HOW FAMOUS VENICE IS, that only around 55,000 people live in the historical city. These are the real Venetians, a small tribe of people who are bound by the autonomy of this authentic and breathtakingly beautiful community. Originally created by refugees, people migrated to this unlikely and remote place in the swamp to avoid wars and persecution. The logic probably being that nobody would follow them to such a forsaken corner of the world. This strategy only partially worked: The isolation certainly didn't last and Venice prospered as a major financial and commercial hub in the Middle Ages and Renaissance while withstanding most challenges and invasions.

Now, Venetians face the greatest challenge of all by modern-day persecutors: the tourists and especially the cruise liners. Though it's a myth that Venetians don't like tourists, they *do* expect the tourists to behave themselves, as you would a guest in your house. A person who stays in town, has meals there, shops, visits museums is one thing. Somebody who barges in with 4,000 others in tow from a cruise ship half the size of the city, for a few hours only, takes selfies, buys nothing, and is not interested in anything but crossing the place off their list, is another thing altogether.

We had somehow, mostly subconsciously, sidestepped Venice through the years, visiting nearly every other place in Italy but this floating city. Either because we were worried it wouldn't measure up to expectations or maybe just because there was always somewhere else to go first. Our first visit could not have been more dramatic. We were going to Friuli for a story that Oddur was working on for *Condé Nast Traveler*. As we often do, we drove from France. Near Lyon, we had a terrible accident, the car flipped over (a dog was involved), and we wound up in a hospital. The choice to continue, with minor yet telling injuries, was a crazy one. We arrived at night, by train. Sailing gently from the station to our hotel, the city seemed deserted and magical. As Oddur wrote in his article, we were like vampires entering a mystical place, not knowing if we were dead or alive. It was in the stillness of late autumn, even more beautiful than I had imagined, misty, quiet. An overall darkness encompassed the city, yet lights and reflections were everywhere, like a thousand prying eyes observing our arrival. I had seen countless pictures of this place, but being there that night felt completely different from what I had imagined, overwhelming and foreign and familiar at once. I have only ever been to Venice in autumn and winter. The Venice I know is a cool place, humid and misty. Quite lively during the day, it's virtually deserted at night and in the early mornings. (Which is also the best time for vampires.) It's a place where during high tide, locals listen out for flood warnings before the crack of dawn, subtle sounds that will inform them how high the water will go and when. A place where flooding is treated like any other routine part of life, and furniture is moved from ground floors to safety without fuss or fear. Fisherman's boots are as much a part of the wardrobe as sunglasses are in Rome. The magic of Venice is that it's a place that is all at once utterly commercial and utterly not. Like the private, secret community of Venetians who live their lives as if they didn't live inside one of the most famous museums in the world. Scurrying from bridge to bridge, disappearing into alleyways, ignoring tourists as if they were ghosts.

There is, of course, far more to Veneto than just Venice itself and the lagoons, which include the islands of Murano, famous for glassblowing, Burano and its legendary lace, and Torcello of Hemingway duck-hunting fame. There is also the beautiful, historical town of Verona; parts of Lake Garda, notably the gorgeous town of Malcesine; Treviso, famous for its bitter, ruby-colored radicchio—the list is long. Veneto is the land of various risottos, cooked with pumpkins, radicchio, even Amarone wine. It's the land of polenta, of Venetian liver, and of various vegetable dishes. Seafood, though, takes top billing: sardines, *baccalà*, stuffed cuttlefish, black ink risotto, various seafood pastas, like *bigoli* with anchovies and onions. The most famous of all dishes from Veneto, though, must be the tiramisù, available everywhere in the world, although these days its status is challenged by the Venetian concoction known as the spritz, also available everywhere in the world.

Our good Italians in Venice are many, even if the inhabitants are few. We have received nothing but warmth everywhere in Italy, but nowhere has it been as surprising and welcome as from the friends we've made in Venice. Gioele Romanelli and his family have run a hotel in Venice for over half a century. That first time we arrived in Venice, half shattered and nearly broken, they showed us a city hidden under the surface. Took us shopping for fish when we feared that all we could find were masks and souvenirs. Cooked with us when we were much happier to eat at home than go to restaurants. Opened doors that might otherwise have been closed, letting us live like locals in the city for a few days. When we think of Venice, we think of the Romanellis (page 193).

Our other good Italians in Venice are the Foscaris, their family history is spun into the history of the city itself. Tracing back forever, the family had several doges (the city's supreme leaders) and commissioned Andrea Palladio, one of the most important architects in history, to build the family a villa in the 1500s. Later, the family lost their wealth and the villa, but in the 1970s, Antonio Foscari and his wife, both architects, bought the villa and painstakingly restored it to its former glory. A renovation job so successful that the villa has been called "the most beautiful house in the world." Antonio's son Ferigo was kind enough to share with us some secret family recipes (page 180), which we cooked with the longstanding family cook, Rosanna, another good Venetian.

# RISOTTO
## WITH PUMPKIN, TREVISO, AND GORGONZOLA FROM THE ROMANELLIS

*Serves 8*

T o us, visiting Venice is visiting the Romanellis—Gioele, Heiby, and their children. They are a wonderful, hotel-owning family that showed us the flip side of Venice on our first visit, the one that tourists seldom get to see. Like us, they love food and wine and family. There is nothing better than going to the market with them in the morning, shopping for fish and vegetables, then cooking together over wine and local starters. We often cook a lovely seafood pasta together at their place, the Casa Flora, but this risotto, also very much in the Venetian tradition, is another favorite. It's one of Heiby's go-to recipes, and the radicchio that plays a big part comes from Gioele's mother's hometown, Treviso.

1   In a large saucepan, bring the stock to a simmer over medium-high heat. Reduce the heat to low to keep the stock at a simmer.

2   In a saucepan, heat 2 tablespoons of the olive oil over medium heat. Add the diced pumpkin and Treviso and season with salt. Cook until softened, 15 to 20 minutes. (You can cook big batches of this and store it in the freezer—very useful for making a quick risotto.) Spoon the mixture into a bowl and set aside. Wipe out the pan.

3   Add the remaining 2 tablespoons olive oil to the saucepan and heat over medium heat. Add the shallots and cook until softened, about 3 minutes. Add the rice and stir well to coat. Sauté for a few minutes. Add a ladle of hot stock along with the pumpkin/Treviso mixture and gently stir. Stir in the turmeric. When the liquid is mostly absorbed, add another ladle of stock, stirring constantly and adding more once each addition is absorbed to keep the rice covered at all times. Repeat this process, stirring constantly, until the rice is creamy but still al dente, 15 to 20 minutes.

4   When the rice is done, stir in the Gorgonzola. Season with salt and serve immediately.

5 CUPS / 1.2 LITERS VEGETABLE STOCK (PAGE 33)

4 TABLESPOONS EXTRA-VIRGIN OLIVE OIL

1 POUND / 500 G PUMPKIN, SEEDED, PEELED, AND CUT INTO SMALL CUBES

4 HEADS RADICCHIO DI TREVISO (ABOUT 1 POUND / 450 G), FINELY CHOPPED

FINE SEA SALT

8 SHALLOTS, FINELY CHOPPED

3 CUPS / 640 G ROSA MARCHETTI RICE (AN ORGANIC MEDIUM-GRAIN RICE) OR ARBORIO OR CARNAROLI RICE

1 TEASPOON GRATED FRESH OR GROUND DRIED TURMERIC

3 OUNCES / 80 G GORGONZOLA CHEESE, CRUMBLED

# RISOTTO
## WITH BABY ARTICHOKES ALLA FRENKY VERGNANO

*Serves 4*

5 CUPS / 1.5 LITERS
VEGETABLE STOCK
(PAGE 33)

12 BABY ARTICHOKES

1 LEMON, HALVED

4 TABLESPOONS
EXTRA-VIRGIN
OLIVE OIL

FINE SEA SALT AND
FRESHLY GROUND
BLACK PEPPER

1 ONION, FINELY
CHOPPED

1½ CUPS / 350 G
CARNAROLI RICE

1 CUP / 90 G FRESHLY
GRATED PARMESAN
CHEESE, PLUS MORE
(OPTIONAL) FOR
SERVING

We love a good coffee almost as much as we love a good glass of wine, so what luck it was to befriend the Vergnanos, the oldest coffee-roasting family in Italy. We've had so much fun together, first tasting coffee, making our own house blend with their single-origin coffee beans, and later just eating and drinking together. The company is run by two brothers, Franco and Carlo, and their grown children, a perfect example of how family is everything in this country, whether in the kitchen or in business. Carolina, Franco's daughter, is a dear friend, and full of fire and fun. We often joke that she's a German Italian; I've never met a more efficient person. Maybe it's all the coffee. The company was founded by Franco's grandfather Domenico, and the family recently converted his home into the Accademia Vergnano, a house of coffee where future baristas can learn their trade. The house also has a beautiful kitchen that we sometimes use for events or workshops. Franco, or Frenky as they call him, is an accomplished cook and does most of the cooking in his house. I had heard from Carolina that her father made the most wonderful risotto, his favorite thing to make. But running a large coffee company means he's also very busy. On the day of the cooking, Carolina and I set the stage, everything was ready. Frenky walked in, calm and elegant, fresh from the boardroom. Took off his jacket and cooked this risotto without a stain or a drop of sweat. Stayed for exactly an hour and then went to the next meeting. Basta. Thanks for sharing, Frenky!

1   In a medium saucepan, bring the vegetable stock to a simmer over medium-high heat. Reduce the heat to low to keep the stock at a simmer.

2   To trim the artichokes, remove the thickest layer of leaves and trim the stems, rubbing them with cut lemon as you go. Cut into slices ¼ inch / 1.25 cm thick.

*(recipe continues)*

3    In a medium saucepan, heat 2 tablespoons of the olive oil over medium heat. Add the artichokes and sauté until crisp-tender, about 5 minutes, seasoning with salt and pepper as you go.

4    In a large, heavy saucepan, heat the remaining 2 tablespoons olive oil over medium heat. Add the onion and cook until translucent and soft, about 3 minutes. Add the rice and stir well to coat. Sauté until nearly toasted, about 2 minutes. Add a ladle of the hot stock along with half of the sautéed artichokes. When the liquid is mostly absorbed, add another ladle of stock, stirring constantly and adding more once each addition is absorbed to keep the rice covered at all times. Repeat this process until the rice is creamy but still al dente, 15 to 20 minutes.

5    Remove the risotto from the heat. Add the Parmesan and the remaining sautéed artichokes, stirring vigorously to make the risotto creamier. Add a small ladle of stock if necessary to adjust the consistency.

6    Serve immediately, adding more grated Parmesan, if desired.

# BONE MARROW RISOTTO

*Serves 4*

2 POUNDS / 1.8 G
BEEF MARROW BONES

FINE SEA SALT

1½ TO 2 QUARTS /
LITERS OXTAIL STOCK
(PAGE 32)

12 TABLESPOONS /
180 G UNSALTED
BUTTER

EXTRA-VIRGIN
OLIVE OIL

4 MEDIUM ONIONS,
FINELY CHOPPED

2 CUPS / 400 G
CARNAROLI RICE

⅔ CUP / 160 ML DRY
WHITE WINE

⅔ CUP /
60 G GRATED
PARMIGIANO-
REGGIANO CHEESE

A FEW FRESH CHIVES,
FINELY CHOPPED

FRESHLY GROUND
BLACK PEPPER

he first time I had this risotto, I said out loud after the first few bites, "This is the best risotto I've ever had." I still stand by that claim, but perhaps it's not fair to compare this risotto to all others, as the old saying about apples and oranges comes to mind. What I typically like about risottos is their freshness and subtlety—and this risotto is anything but. It's intensely flavorful, salty, thick, and heavy. If regular risottos are light jazz, this bone marrow version is rock 'n' roll.

This is an original recipe from Consorzio, one of the very best restaurants in Torino. I'm grateful to the guys, Pietro especially, for sharing it with me; we had such fun photographing and eating this wonderful risotto. And even if I now know all the secrets behind it, I still make sure that at least one person at my table orders it when we go to Consorzio, so I can have a spoon or two. Or three.

1 The day before, in a large bowl, combine the marrow bones with water to cover and 3 tablespoons salt. Refrigerate and soak for 24 hours. Change the water two or three times in that period, adding more salt each time.

2 Pat the bones dry and remove the marrow with a long spoon. Cut into 12 slices, each about ¾ inch / 2 cm thick. Set aside.

3 In a medium saucepan, bring the stock to a simmer over medium-high heat. Reduce the heat to low to keep the stock at a simmer.

4 In a large sauté pan, heat 6 tablespoons of the butter, 2 tablespoons olive oil, a pinch of salt, and half the bone marrow over medium heat. When it begins to melt and sizzle, add the onions, then cover and cook for 5 minutes. Uncover and continue to cook until the onions have softened completely, another 5 minutes. Set the onion *soffritto* aside.

5   In a large, heavy saucepan, heat 2 tablespoons olive oil over medium
    heat. Add the rice and stir well to coat. Sauté until the oil has coated
    the rice evenly, about 3 minutes. Stir in 1 teaspoon salt and three-
    quarters of the onion *soffritto*. Stir in the white wine. When the
    wine starts to evaporate, gradually begin adding the hot stock by the
    ladleful, stirring constantly, adding more to keep the rice covered at all
    times. Repeat this step until the rice is creamy but still al dente, 15 to
    20 minutes.

6   Preheat the broiler. Place the remaining marrow on a baking sheet
    with the remaining onion *soffritto* on top. Broil until sizzling, about
    5 minutes.

7   Remove the risotto from the heat and add the Parmigiano and the
    remaining 6 tablespoons butter. Stir well until you get a creamy
    mixture. Divide among serving dishes and top with the broiled bone
    marrow and a scattering of finely chopped chives. Season with salt and
    pepper and serve immediately.

ONE OF THE BIGGEST CLICHÉS ABOUT MILANO IS THAT IT'S NOT A beautiful city. Probably in comparison to the more striking beauty of Florence and Rome, it's regarded as gray, cold, closed off. But it's also true that beneath the stern exterior are some hidden treasures and secret gardens if one could only find them. I have always found Milano a joy to visit, and beautiful, too. Besides, it's not really fair to compare every city to Rome; it's almost like saying a woman can't be beautiful if she doesn't look like Sophia Loren. Milano is a powerhouse, the center of finance and fashion in Italy. No city has more or greater energy in the arts and design, and I'm told it's a lovely place to live. Easily the most international city in Italy, it also has a long history of wealth and prosperity, which in turn gives it a great gastronomic heritage, a tale of spare-no-expense cuisine. The lords of Milano were obsessed with the color of gold, a symbol of nobility. As such, they commissioned a golden cuisine to match their ambition and status: Egg yolk was one way to achieve this desired hue, saffron another. The most iconic dish of Milano is without a doubt *risotto alla milanese*, a bright-yellow, creamy, and delicious rice dish that's either served on its own or with osso buco, which is unusual since risottos are almost always served before meat and without company. The Milanese way is to cook with rice and butter rather than olive oil and pasta. The most famous culinary export of the city though, found on the menu of almost every Italian restaurant, even in Italy, is the crispy, breaded *cotoletta milanese*, a veal cutlet traditionally fried with the bone still attached, unlike, say, Wiener schnitzel, which is boneless.

And lastly, another famous golden creation of Milano is panettone, the traditional fruit-studded bread available everywhere in Italy around the holidays (and might I add, on our table every single morning throughout December).

On a memorable trip to Milano some thirteen years ago, my luggage got lost and my hotel room was not ready. I had on a cashmere turtleneck with no other clothes to wear, and I was too stubborn to buy something for the sake of it. It was June and it was hot. I remember spending the morning doing restaurant research in the hotel lobby and finding an old article written by Mimi Sheraton for the *New York Times*. She was recommending a number of the most classic restaurants in the city. She also recommended a gourmet store called Peck, which was perfect for my condition, as gourmet stores tend to

be suitable climates for turtlenecks. Peck is a huge, glamorous, opulent food emporium. Perfect for a distressed woman in love with food, killing time, fantasizing about a glass of red wine and a big piece of Gorgonzola. So I went there and had exactly that and, feeling better, even bought myself a little dress. Sometimes you need some wine and cheese to make the right decision. Over the next few days, we went to all of Mimi's restaurants and liked them all. Some are still my favorite restaurants in Milano. One of them, Antica Trattoria della Pesa (see page 206), is one of my favorite restaurants in the world. Thank you, Mimi, I owe you one.

Milano is many things, a mix of different types of architecture from different eras. I love the 1930s buildings, so clean and functional and beautiful. If I had only a few hours in Milano, I would take a taxi to Villa Necchi, once home to a wealthy Milanese family but now a museum. I would maybe get myself a pair of Porselli ballet flats at the original store near La Scala. And hunt for some vintage finds in via Brera nearby, at Cavalli e Nastri. I might have lunch at Latteria, also in Brera, a tiny little place where a husband and wife take care of a handful of guests every lunch and dinner. The cooking is simple and so is the place. He cooks everything on an old silver pan, which adds some . . . luster to the cooking. Before dinner, I'd have drinks at Bar Basso, a quirky, busy bar in a residential area. Either very quiet or very full, the mood is interesting and appropriate. I'm not a big fan of the Italian *aperitivi,* being more of a Champagne kind of girl, but here, it's a must to have one—a *sbagliato,* which means "mistake" in Italian; as in the mistake of adding Prosecco to a Negroni instead of gin (which actually happened for real at Bar Basso in Milan, thus the name of the drink). The following morning, I might drive up to Lake Como; it's not far, only about an hour. If the time was right, I might have lunch in Como town, but if not, I'd continue the drive, a magical, slightly scary drive alongside the lake, from village to village, where the roads are designed for one vehicle but have to accommodate two that pass. I'd end up in Tremezzo, where Greta Garbo once stayed. I'd check in at the Grand Hotel, have lunch, and swim in the lake. And I would say to myself: It feels like I'm in Italy.

# RISOTTO MILANESE

*Serves 2*

2 CUPS / 500 ML
OXTAIL STOCK
(PAGE 32) OR
BEEF STOCK

5½ TABLESPOONS /
80 G UNSALTED
BUTTER

1 MEDIUM ONION,
AS FINELY CHOPPED
AS POSSIBLE

1 CUP / 200 G
CARNAROLI RICE

½ TEASPOON
SAFFRON THREADS

2 TABLESPOONS DRY
WHITE WINE

GENEROUS ½ CUP /
50 G GRATED
PARMIGIANO-
REGGIANO CHEESE

A ntica Trattoria della Pesa is without a doubt our favorite restaurant in Milano. We've been going there for over a decade, and every time we go to Milano, we feel the need to visit again. Revisiting the same restaurant may seem narrow-minded and stubborn, but it's not about that. When you find, finally, exactly what you were always looking for, why look further? The restaurant is beautiful, neither overdone nor overly conceptual. The décor is just right. The waiters have been there for years, which speaks volumes for the Sassi family that runs the trattoria. The wine list is good for a trattoria, the menu has everything I want to eat in a traditional Milanese restaurant, and all of it feels like home cooking. Osso buco, *cotoletta milanese, zabaione,* and, obviously, saffron risotto. This is not a fussy version, no unusual flavors, no inventiveness. It's *risotto alla milanese* just how it should be.

Francesca Gaia, the proprietor's daughter, is always at the restaurant when her father is not, and she was very happy, after all these years, to share a few recipes. Unlike some versions of *risotto alla milanese,* theirs uses no bone marrow, but they use a rich beef stock instead. *Risotto al salto* is the same risotto, but pan-fried after cooling down. This is a traditional way of using leftover risotto; you don't always find it in restaurants, which is why I always order it there.

1   In a medium saucepan, bring the stock to a simmer over medium-high heat. Reduce the heat to low to keep the stock at a simmer.

2   In a large, heavy saucepan, heat half of the butter over medium heat. Add the onion and sweat until softened, about 3 minutes. Add the rice, saffron threads, and wine and stir with a wooden spoon. Cook until the wine is absorbed, about 2 minutes.

3   Gradually begin adding the hot stock by the ladleful, stirring constantly, adding more to keep the rice covered at all times. Repeat this process until the rice is creamy but still al dente, 15 to 20 minutes.

4   Remove the risotto from the heat. Add the remaining butter and the Parmigiano, stirring vigorously to make the risotto creamier. Serve immediately.

### RISOTTO AL SALTO
#### Pan-Fried Risotto

*Serves 1*

3½ TABLESPOONS / 50 G UNSALTED BUTTER

½ CUP / 110 G LEFTOVER RISOTTO MILANESE (OPPOSITE), CHILLED

In a small skillet, heat 2 tablespoons / 30 g of the butter over medium heat. When the butter is sizzling, add the risotto and flatten with a wooden spoon into a disk about ½ inch / 1.25 cm thick. Cook until golden, about 3 minutes. Slide the risotto onto a plate and add the remaining 1½ tablespoons / 20 g butter to the pan. Heat again until the butter is sizzling and cook the other side of the risotto disk until golden, another 3 minutes. Flip onto a plate and serve immediately.

# *SECONDI*

his is the money part. Respect. How much you value your guests. They enjoyed the starters, the wine is nice, the pasta was delightful. Really. But this is the measure of the meal. How far will you go, where are you taking this? A simple veal for family, or something more. Lobster, the thickest steak. Something unusual or hard to get. Now, we're back where we began. Like the antipasti, it's all about investment. How exclusive is the protein involved: Is it luxurious or is it just good? I'm half-kidding, of course. But only half. This part is very much about presentation; you might not need it, but you want it. I love Italian cooking best when a piece of meat is used to the maximum of its potential. First to flavor a sauce, then served on its own. So very ceremonial. Revered, like meat should always be if you serve it at all. Animals should never be served without ceremony. They're different from all other ingredients and should be appreciated like they were in the old days when nobody ever had much. The *secondi* course of Italian dining is a celebration, not a necessity, a way of saying thank you for serving, to the host and to the beast. Presentation is important, an oval porcelain plate, some herbs for garnish, and small portions. And everyone appreciates each bite. The opposite of mindless eating is thoughtful eating. That's what the second course of Italian dining is to me—historical catches up with contemporary, and wasteful is off the table forever.

# CALAMARI RIPIENI
## CON RADICCHIO DI TREVISO E NOCI FROM CORTE SCONTA
### *Stuffed Squid with Radicchio and Walnuts*

*Serves 4*

6 MEDIUM TO LARGE
SQUID (ABOUT
1½ POUNDS /
680 G), CLEANED,
TENTACLES
SEPARATED

7 TABLESPOONS
EXTRA-VIRGIN
OLIVE OIL

4 GARLIC CLOVES,
MINCED

FINE SEA SALT

4 SHALLOTS, FINELY
DICED

5 OUNCES / 150 G
RADICCHIO DI
TREVISO, FINELY
CHOPPED, PLUS A
FEW THINLY SLICED
LEAVES FOR GARNISH

4 CUPS PLUS
2 TABLESPOONS /
1 LITER RABOSO
OR OTHER FULL-
BODIED, TANNIC
RED WINE

FRESHLY GROUND
BLACK PEPPER

enice is actually a cluster of islands in a lagoon on the Adriatic Sea, so it's natural that traditional Venetian cuisine is mostly based around fish and other seafood from the lagoons. The region also has a rich hunting heritage that translates to the table, especially in home cooking. The local vegetable production is legendary, too, not least the artichokes and beautiful radicchio. Adding to this, Venetians were by nature merchants, and very good at it, too, so they were often in a position to buy exotic ingredients and produce from other regions. All this makes Venetian cuisine quite varied and very interesting. However, when I chose the recipes from Venice to include in the book, I wanted the emphasis to be on seafood, with a strong hint of radicchio. This recipe from Corte Sconta has both and is distinctively Venetian. The red wine is a bit of a surprise, but it works very well and elevates the dish.

1   Chop 2 of the squid (including the tentacles) as finely as possible. In a large sauté pan, heat 2 tablespoons of the olive oil and the garlic over medium heat. Add the chopped squid and tentacles and season with salt. Cook, stirring frequently, until cooked through, about 5 minutes. Transfer the chopped squid mixture to a large bowl and set aside.

2   In the same pan, add 3 tablespoons of the olive oil over medium heat. Add the shallots and radicchio and sauté until golden and softened, about 5 minutes. Add 2 tablespoons of the red wine and reduce for 1 minute. Season with salt and pepper.

3   Add the shallot/radicchio mixture to the bowl with the chopped squid. Add the walnuts and mashed potatoes and mix well. Check the filling for seasoning. Using a teaspoon, put some filling inside the 4 remaining squid, taking care not to overstuff. Secure each calamari with a toothpick.

4 Arrange the stuffed calamari in a Dutch oven. Season the calamari on both sides with salt and pepper and drizzle with the remaining 2 tablespoons olive oil. Add the tentacles and season with salt and pepper. Pour in the remaining 4 cups / 950 ml red wine. Bring to a boil over medium heat, then cover and cook until tender, about 25 minutes. Use a slotted spoon to transfer the cooked squid to a plate and cover to keep warm.

5 In a small bowl, combine the butter and cornstarch and mix until a smooth paste forms. Return the Dutch oven to medium heat. Add the mixture to the sauce and cook, stirring constantly, over medium heat. When the sauce is glossy and starts to thicken, remove from the heat.

6 Divide the calamari among serving plates. Garnish each with a few strips of the radicchio as if they were tentacles, scatter chopped parsley all over, and drizzle with the sauce. Serve hot.

½ CUP / 80 G WALNUTS, LIGHTLY TOASTED AND FINELY CHOPPED

5 OUNCES / 150 G MASHED POTATOES

2 TABLESPOONS / 30 G UNSALTED BUTTER, AT ROOM TEMPERATURE

¼ CUP / 30 G CORNSTARCH

2 TABLESPOONS CHOPPED FRESH PARSLEY, FOR GARNISH

# *POLPETTE DI SOPHIA LOREN*
### *Meatballs in Cream Sauce*

*Serves 4*

1 CUP / 250 ML
WHOLE MILK

4 THICK (½ INCH /
1.25 CM) SLICES
STALE WHITE BREAD,
CRUSTS REMOVED

1 POUND / 450 G
GROUND BEEF

FINE SEA SALT AND
FRESHLY GROUND
BLACK PEPPER

ALL-PURPOSE FLOUR,
FOR DREDGING

EXTRA-VIRGIN OLIVE
OIL, FOR FRYING

⅓ CUP / 80 ML
WHITE WINE

¼ CUP / 60 ML
CHICKEN STOCK
(SEE PAGE 33)

1 CUP / 250 ML
HEAVY CREAM

A HANDFUL OF
CHOPPED FRESH
PARSLEY

MASHED POTATOES,
FOR SERVING

 his recipe is very meaningful to me, and it comes with a story. And that story starts, of all places, in Iceland. In winter. Which is about as far away as you can get from Napoli—maybe not in distance, but in everything else. We were spending time in Reykjavik, and when the weather is unkind there, as it often is, people flock to the bookstores where they drink lattes, eat pastries, and read magazines and books. On such a day, to my surprise, I found a cookbook by one of my all-time favorite icons, Sophia Loren. I had no idea that she was into cooking, but of course I bought it; it was beautiful and the recipes looked delicious. It made my day—and became the most important cookbook I've ever bought, full of recipes and memories. Who would have thought that such a captivating actress was also such an accomplished cook. (Of course, she's Italian, from Napoli, so that explains a lot.) Needless to say, the recipes are wonderful, as are the stories. You may admire this woman for her movie roles and her style, but to me, this book reveals who she really is, an Italian woman with a flair for everything, including cooking. I've cooked this meal so often since then; her boys loved it as children and my entire family is in love with it, even my father-in-law.

1  In a medium bowl, combine the milk and bread. Set aside and let the bread completely absorb the milk.

2  Squeeze the excess milk from the bread and place the bread in a large bowl. Add the ground beef, season with salt and pepper, and mix to combine evenly. Shape into meatballs 1½ to 2 inches / 4 to 5 cm in diameter.

3  Add flour to a shallow bowl and dredge the meatballs lightly in the flour.

4  Pour about ¾ inch / 2 cm olive oil into a large, heavy sauté pan and heat over medium heat. Working in batches, fry the meatballs until golden brown all over, about 6 minutes. Drain on a plate lined with paper towels.

MEAT & SEAFOOD

5   Pour off the excess oil from the skillet and scrape off any residue. Add the wine and cook over medium-high heat until it reduces by one-quarter. Add the chicken stock and cream, reduce the heat to low, and cook for 1 minute. Return the meatballs to the pan, making sure all the meatballs are covered in the sauce. Do not let the sauce boil or the cream will start separating.

6   Transfer the meatballs to a serving platter or individual plates. Sprinkle with parsley, serve with mashed potatoes, and drizzle lots of sauce on top.

## TOMATO SAUCE

⅓ CUP / 80 ML
EXTRA-VIRGIN
OLIVE OIL

1 MEDIUM RED
ONION, DICED

2 GARLIC CLOVES,
MINCED

¼ TEASPOON
CRUSHED RED
PEPPER FLAKES

17.6 OUNCES
(1½ CUPS) / 500 G
CHOPPED TOMATOES,
DRAINED

½ CUP / 120 ML
RED WINE

1 TABLESPOON
TOMATO PASTE

1 TEASPOON DRIED
OREGANO

FINE SEA SALT AND
FRESHLY GROUND
BLACK PEPPER

## MEATBALLS

½ POUND / 230 G
GROUND BEEF

½ POUND / 230 G
GROUND PORK

1 SMALL ONION,
FINELY CHOPPED

1 CUP / 65 G FRESH
BREAD CRUMBS

2 GARLIC CLOVES,
MINCED

# POLPETTE AL FORNO
## CON MOZZARELLA
### Baked Meatballs with Tomato Sauce and Mozzarella

 t goes without saying that this is a family favorite, and not just mine, as I suspect that meatballs in tomato sauce are high on everybody's list. Unlike the American classic, spaghetti and meatballs, meatballs are never served with pasta in Italy, but rather on their own as a second course, often with roast potatoes or spinach or both. The melted mozzarella adds a juicy finish, and while it's not necessary, it's definitely an improvement. It's not a question of why, but why not!

1   **Make the tomato sauce:** In a large Dutch oven or flameproof casserole, heat the olive oil over medium-low heat. Add the onion and cook until tender, about 6 minutes. Add the garlic and pepper flakes and cook until softened, about 2 minutes. Stir in the tomatoes, red wine, tomato paste, and oregano. Season with salt and pepper. Reduce the heat to a simmer, cover, and cook, stirring occasionally, until thickened, about 30 minutes.

2   Preheat the oven to 350°F / 180°C.

3   **Make the meatballs:** Crumble the ground beef and pork into a large bowl. Add the onion, bread crumbs, garlic, oregano, cream, egg, parsley, and Parmesan and mix to combine evenly. Season with salt and pepper. Shape into meatballs about 1½ inches / 4 cm in diameter.

4   Add flour to a bowl and lightly dredge the meatballs in the flour.

5   In a large skillet, heat the olive oil over medium-high heat. Working in batches, brown the meatballs on all sides, about 5 minutes. Set the meatballs aside on a plate.

6   **Assemble the dish:** Transfer the meatballs to the simmering tomato sauce and top with the mozzarella slices. Sprinkle the Parmesan all over. Drizzle with a little olive oil and transfer to the oven.

7   Bake until bubbling and golden, about 45 minutes. Serve hot, sprinkled with parsley.

1 TEASPOON DRIED
OREGANO

2 TABLESPOONS
HEAVY CREAM

1 LARGE EGG,
LIGHTLY BEATEN

A SMALL HANDFUL
OF FRESH PARSLEY,
FINELY CHOPPED

⅔ CUP / 60 G FINELY
GRATED PARMESAN
CHEESE

FINE SEA SALT AND
FRESHLY GROUND
BLACK PEPPER

ALL-PURPOSE FLOUR,
FOR DREDGING

¼ CUP / 60 ML
EXTRA-VIRGIN OLIVE
OIL, FOR FRYING

*ASSEMBLY*

9 OUNCES / 250 G
MOZZARELLA
CHEESE (ABOUT
2 MOZZARELLA
BALLS), THICKLY
SLICED

1 CUP / 120 G GRATED
PARMESAN CHEESE

EXTRA-VIRGIN OLIVE
OIL, FOR DRIZZLING

CHOPPED FRESH
PARSLEY, FOR
GARNISH

SECONDI

# BACCALÀ
## WITH POTATOES

One of my favorite rituals to watch is Andrea Vannelli from Al Gatto Nero preparing this dish at the side of the kitchen, in his graceful, serene way. He stands there in his white jacket, carefully folding the fish in with the potatoes as if he were boning a fish or preparing duck. This dish, kiddie food for grown-ups, is simplicity itself, and the olive oil is absolutely key.

1  Cut the salt cod into large chunks and put them in a large bowl. Add enough water to cover. Put the cod in the refrigerator and let it soak for 48 hours, changing the water at least four times a day.

2  In a medium saucepan, combine 2 quarts / liters water with the onion, garlic, and bay leaf. Bring to a boil. Add the salt cod and cover. Remove from the heat and let the fish sit in the water just until it can be pulled apart with a fork, 10 to 15 minutes. Use tongs to remove the cod. Reserve the water.

3  When the fish is cool enough to handle, pick out any bones and remove the skin. Use a fork to flake the fish.

4  Bring the water back to a boil. Add the potatoes and cook until very tender, about 25 minutes. Drain.

5  Transfer the cod and potatoes to a large bowl and mash with the fork, adding the olive oil while mashing until you get a creamy texture.

6  Place a palm-size ring mold on each serving plate and add the potato and cod mixture. Lift the ring and drizzle the disk with olive oil just before serving.

*Serves 4 to 6*

1 POUND / 450 G
BACCALÀ (SALT COD)

1 MEDIUM ONION,
QUARTERED

1 GARLIC CLOVE,
HALVED

1 BAY LEAF

12 OUNCES / 350 G
WAXY POTATOES,
PEELED AND
QUARTERED

¾ CUP / 180 ML
EXTRA-VIRGIN
OLIVE OIL,
PLUS MORE FOR
DRIZZLING

# CAPPONE DI NATALE RIPIENO
## CON SALSICCIA DI BRA

*Christmas Roast Capon with Chestnuts, Marsala, and Bra Sausage*

*Serves 6*

**STUFFED CAPON**

1 WHOLE CAPON
(4½ POUNDS /
2 KG), ENTIRELY
DEBONED (ASK
YOUR BUTCHER TO
PREPARE)

2¼ POUNDS / 1 KG
CHESTNUTS, COOKED
AND PEELED

1 SLICE STALE BREAD,
CRUST REMOVED,
TORN INTO PIECES

⅓ CUP / 80 ML
WHOLE MILK

10 OUNCES / 300 G
GROUND PORK

½ POUND / 230 G
BRA (VEAL) SAUSAGE,
CASINGS REMOVED

2 LARGE EGGS

1 CUP PLUS
2 TABLESPOONS /
100 G GRATED
PARMESAN CHEESE

⅓ CUP / 80 ML DRY
MARSALA WINE

Italians like to eat fish during the holidays, but like in many other countries, Italian Christmas traditions often involve stuffed birds. This is the recipe I cooked last Christmas, with a Piedmontese touch. A fatty bird stuffed with goodness, including chestnuts (one of my favorite foods), Marsala from Sicily that adds sweetness, and Bra sausages, famous for their flavor and quality and made from lean veal and a little bacon.

1  **Prepare the stuffed capon:** Preheat the oven to 350°F / 180°C.

2  Clean the capon and pat dry.

3  Place half of the chestnuts in a bowl, mash them with a fork, and set aside.

4  In a small bowl, combine the bread and the milk and soak until softened. Squeeze out the excess milk.

5  In a large bowl, combine the ground pork, sausage meat, and soaked bread. Add the eggs, Parmesan, Marsala, sage, mashed chestnuts, and nutmeg. Season with salt and pepper. Mix well.

6  Lay the capon skin side down on a work surface and spread the filling over the flesh, then roll up, starting from a long side. Wrap the top part of the rolled capon horizontally with the pancetta. Tie the roast in several places with kitchen twine. In a roasting pan large enough to hold the bird, drizzle a little olive oil. Place the rolled bird in the center of the roasting pan and drizzle with more olive oil. Season with salt and pepper. Dot the bird with the butter.

7  Transfer to the oven and roast, basting the bird regularly, until cooked through, about 2 hours. About 15 minutes before the end of cooking, add the remaining chestnuts to the roasting pan. Transfer the bird to a cutting board and the chestnuts to a bowl, cover the bird with foil, and let rest for 10 minutes.

8   **Meanwhile, make the gravy:** Place the roasting pan over medium heat. Add the wine and deglaze the pan, stirring constantly. Scrape up all of the browned bits and bring to a boil. Add 3 tablespoons butter. When the butter is melted, add the sifted cornstarch and whisk it into the sauce. Cook until glossy and thickened, about 5 minutes. Season with salt and pepper.

9   Carve the capon into slices ¾ inch / 2 cm thick and serve with the gravy and chestnuts on the side.

NOTE: *Instead of capon, you can also make this recipe with a chicken or a turkey, adjusting the stuffing amounts and cooking time. For the Bra sausage, you can use an herbed pork sausage.*

12 FRESH SAGE
LEAVES, FINELY
CHOPPED

1 TEASPOON GRATED
NUTMEG

FINE SEA SALT AND
FRESHLY GROUND
BLACK PEPPER

4 OUNCES / 140 G
PANCETTA, SLICED
(ABOUT 20 PIECES),
OR THINLY SLICED
BACON

EXTRA-VIRGIN
OLIVE OIL

2 TABLESPOONS /
30 G UNSALTED
BUTTER, AT ROOM
TEMPERATURE

*GRAVY*

⅔ CUP / 160 ML
WHITE WINE

3 TABLESPOONS /
45 G UNSALTED
BUTTER

1 TABLESPOON
CORNSTARCH, SIFTED

FINE SEA SALT AND
FRESHLY GROUND
BLACK PEPPER

# BRANZINO AL SALE

*Branzino Baked in a Salt Crust*

his is a remarkably simple way to cook fish that's perfectly seasoned and moist when you remove it from the crust. I'm sure many of you will balk at the thought of cooking a fish whole, but it's a fear worth getting over, and one of the easiest things you'll ever do.

Fish in salt crust is also one of the most visually enchanting recipes I can think of and reminds us of the Amalfi Coast, where we have spent many vacations. It became a beacon for us, a symbolic dish that represented all that was good about Italy. We'd be in Iceland or Paris in the midst of winter and Oddur would say, "Close your eyes. Imagine you're in Amalfi and in front of you is white fish with salty crust. You slice a lemon, squeeze it over the fish, and with the other hand you reach for the white wine." It's that sort of dish.

1   Preheat the oven to 420°F / 240°C.

2   Wash the fish and pat dry.

3   On a large rimmed baking sheet, use a little less than half the salt to form a bed for the fish. Place the fish on top. Stuff the cavity with the sliced lemons, bay leaves, and fennel. Pour the rest of the salt over and around the fish so the fish is entirely covered. Spray a little water on top of the salt so that it becomes more compact, gently pressing down with your palms if necessary.

4   Transfer to the oven and roast for 30 minutes. Remove from the oven and let rest for 10 minutes.

5   To serve, crack the salt crust with a large spoon and pull it away from the fish. Serve the fish with a drizzle of olive oil, a scattering of fennel or tarragon, and extra lemon on the side. If you want to impress your guests, you can take the pan directly to the table and break the salt layer right in front of them.

*Serves 4 to 6*

1 WHOLE BRANZINO
(3 POUNDS 5 OUNCES /
1.5 KG), CLEANED
(YOU CAN ASK YOUR
FISHMONGER TO DO
IT FOR YOU)

4 TO 6 POUNDS /
2 TO 3 KG COARSE SEA
SALT

2 LEMONS, SLICED,
PLUS MORE FOR
SERVING

3 BAY LEAVES

½ CUP / 25 G
CHOPPED FENNEL
FRONDS OR
TARRAGON, PLUS
MORE FOR GARNISH

EXTRA-VIRGIN OLIVE
OIL, FOR DRIZZLING

# CHICKEN SUPREME

*Serves 6*

5 TABLESPOONS /
75 ML EXTRA-VIRGIN
OLIVE OIL

6 CHICKEN BREAST
QUARTERS
(BONE-IN, SKIN-ON
BREASTS WITH WINGS
ATTACHED)

FINE SEA SALT AND
FRESHLY GROUND
BLACK PEPPER

1 CAN (16 OUNCES /
450 G) CANNELLINI
BEANS, RINSED AND
DRAINED

A BUNCH OF FRESH
ROSEMARY

8 GARLIC CLOVES,
UNPEELED AND
LIGHTLY SMASHED

⅔ CUP / 160 ML DRY
WHITE WINE

This dish is in the details. On the face of it, we are just talking about pan-fried chicken, finished in the oven with some cannellini beans, garlic, rosemary, and a generous drizzle of olive oil. Wait, that doesn't sound half bad does it? It does get better though. This cut of chicken has two advantages: The wing bone is attached, which makes for a juicier result than a boneless breast would usually give you, and the skin is kept on so you get that all-important salty, crunchy texture. If you can't find the chicken breast with the wing still attached, feel free to use the regular bone-in, skin-on variety.

1   Preheat the oven to 350°F / 180°C.

2   Drizzle 2 tablespoons of the olive oil over the chicken breast quarters and season with salt and pepper. Heat a large, heavy sauté pan over medium-high heat and add 2 tablespoons of the olive oil. Add the chicken, skin side down. Once the skin is golden, about 3 minutes, flip the breasts and brown the other side, about 2 minutes. Remove from the heat.

3   Scatter the beans in a large roasting pan or baking dish and place the breasts skin side up on top. Drizzle with all the juices from the sauté pan. Scatter some rosemary sprigs and the garlic all over, add the white wine, and season lightly with salt and pepper. Drizzle with the remaining tablespoon olive oil. Roast until cooked through, 12 to 15 minutes, depending on thickness of breasts.

4   To serve, place the chicken on a serving plate and spoon the beans on top. Garnish with rosemary.

A FEW YEARS AGO, WE HAD BEEN TO UMBRIA ONLY ONCE. A DAY
trip from Marche to Perugia, where we had spent a couple of vacations. We
had often been nearby, in Tuscany, so close but never crossed the border,
although the idea went through our minds. Then Oddur was commissioned to
photograph the fashion designer Brunello Cucinelli for *Condé Nast Traveler*. He
took two of our boys and the whole trip was a revelation. I remember Oddur
describing the region as the perfect part of Italy. He still says that if he ever
loses me, he'll go live alone in Umbria with his dogs. It's become one of our
favorite regions in Italy (I say that a lot, don't I?) and we've been back a dozen
times in the last few years. The rolling hills, the cypress trees, the mountains,
and the beautiful valleys. It's Tuscany toned down, without (most of) the tourists. They've got heartwarming cuisine and incredibly varied settings. Baroque
meets brick, peasant meets posh, and the most stunning olive groves I've ever
seen in my life. Umbria is a relatively small region, right in the middle of Italy,
bordering the far more famous and larger regions of Tuscany and Lazio.

Umbria's greatest contribution to Italian cuisine is undoubtedly in the
field of cured meats. Stretching back centuries, and to this day, Norcia, a
small town in the southeastern part of Umbria, is considered a benchmark
for Italian *salumi*. The meats are so revered that the word in Italy for a butcher
that specializes in charcuterie comes from the name of the town—*norcino*—
and a place that sells Umbrian-style pork products, anywhere in Italy, is called
a *norcineria*. Nearby, Castelluccio, the sole village of Umbria's great plains, is
well known for its excellent lentils, another Umbrian staple. Umbrian cuisine
is the cooking of farmers and hunters. Game, especially wild boar, plays a
huge part in local cooking and also in the cured meat traditions. The region
is rich with pigeons and pheasants, even snails. It's the land of hearty fare,
including bean stews and farro soup, gnocchi with sausage, hunter's chicken
(the Umbrian version is without tomatoes), and sausage bakes. Umbria is
also the largest producer of black truffles, which are not as well-known as the
white truffles of Piemonte, but often (almost) as delicious and certainly more
affordable. Perugia, the regional capital, is one of Italy's cities of chocolate, a
beautiful hilltop town with a medieval cultural heritage. From Perugia, there
is a clear, beautiful view of Assisi, the birthplace of St. Francis, a patron saint

of Italy; and from the hills stretches the Valle Umbra, a glorious green valley, one of the country's most beautiful. Umbria is a place that has preserved its traditions without relying on other regions for supplies. It's mostly avoided large-scale farming and is therefore perfectly suited to the modern ways of thinking, meaning smaller, better producers and green approaches that are artisanal rather than mass market.

My good Italians in Umbria are some of the most interesting, loveliest people you'll ever meet. Nencia and Benedikt Bolza: She's Italian, he's Austro-Hungarian, and neither is native to Umbria. Both have aristocratic backgrounds: She's a Corsini from Florence, one of the city's oldest ruling families, and he's from a family of Hungarian counts. His father, Antonio, fled communism, leaving behind the family fortune, but he made a new one in publishing in Germany. He got tired of vacationing in Forte dei Marmi, fell in love with Umbria, and ended up buying a large part of it when prices were favorable in the '90s. The whole family is in love with their property at Reschio in the northern part of Umbria near the Tuscan border. Benedikt, who is an architect, has been developing the property for most of his adult life, selling small parts of it to like-minded people who want a vacation home in this beautiful place. The Bolzas transformed the land, rebuilding and selling various forlorn structures and putting badly needed infrastructure in place. Now, they are taking the whole thing further by building an ambitious hotel in their castello, two restaurants, and the most magnificent equestrian theater. One of my favorite things about visiting Reschio is that it's at once completely elegant and beautiful but also very natural to its setting. The land feels so unspoiled, as everything is done with respect for nature, whether it's farming or hunting. Nencia and Benedikt take great pride in their synergic garden; most or all the produce on their table is homegrown. Nencia is in love with peppers, especially the spicy little ones. At lunch or dinner, each guest has his own fresh pepper and the cutest pair of scissors to cut off as much or little as needed to blend into their food. And putting a twist on the classic Bloody Mary (see page 45), the Bolzas make theirs with peppers instead of tomatoes, which is interesting and delicious to me, not least because they grow the peppers themselves.

# SCALOPPINE ALLA PERUGINA

### Veal Scaloppine with Chicken Liver, Anchovies, and Capers

When I think of Italian *secondi* (main courses), what come most frequently to mind are scaloppine, the thinly sliced veal cuts that are available, in some form, in almost every restaurant. The best known versions are probably with lemon or Marsala sauce, the pizzaiola version with tomato, or the saltimbocca (page 230). This is a more obscure Umbrian version, with the unlikely marriage of anchovies, capers, and chicken livers. The result is a rustic, gamy, flavorful dish that evokes scenes of sitting by the fireplace in an Umbrian farmhouse, today or a hundred years ago. The lemon zest adds a hint of modernity and a touch of brightness.

1  In a medium sauté pan, heat 2 tablespoons olive oil over medium heat. Add the prosciutto, anchovies, chicken liver, garlic, and sage and cook until the mixture is browned, about 3 minutes. Add the capers, lemon zest, and lemon juice. Stir constantly until all the ingredients are combined and soft. Season with salt and pepper. Add half of the white wine and let reduce for 1 to 2 minutes. Add 1 tablespoon of the butter and mix well. Set aside and keep warm.

2  Add flour to a shallow bowl and dredge the veal cutlets in the flour. Shake off the excess.

3  In a large sauté pan, heat 4 tablespoons olive oil and the remaining 1 tablespoon butter over high heat. Add the veal in batches and cook until golden brown, 1 minute on each side. Add the remaining wine and let reduce for 1 minute. Season with pepper.

4  Divide the veal among serving plates and place the prosciutto mixture on top. Pour the sauce on top, scatter with the chopped parsley leaves if you like, and serve.

### Serves 4

EXTRA-VIRGIN OLIVE OIL

4 OUNCES / 110 G PROSCIUTTO, FINELY DICED

3 OIL-PACKED ANCHOVY FILLETS, FINELY CHOPPED

1 CHICKEN LIVER, CHOPPED AS FINELY AS POSSIBLE

1 GARLIC CLOVE, MINCED

8 FRESH SAGE LEAVES, FINELY CHOPPED

1 TABLESPOON CAPERS

GRATED ZEST AND JUICE OF ½ LEMON

FINE SEA SALT AND FRESHLY GROUND BLACK PEPPER

⅓ CUP / 80 ML WHITE WINE

2 TABLESPOONS / 28G UNSALTED BUTTER

ALL-PURPOSE FLOUR, FOR DREDGING

1 POUND / 450 G THINLY SLICED VEAL CUTLETS

SECONDI

# SALTIMBOCCA ALLA ROMANA
### Veal Scaloppine with Sage and Prosciutto

*Serves 4*

8 SLICES VEAL
CUTLETS (1 POUND /
450 G TOTAL)

FINE SEA SALT AND
FRESHLY GROUND
BLACK PEPPER

½ CUP / 60 G
CORNSTARCH, FOR
DUSTING

8 THIN SLICES
PROSCIUTTO

A BUNCH OF FRESH
SAGE, LEAVES PICKED

4 TABLESPOONS
EXTRA-VIRGIN
OLIVE OIL

3 TABLESPOONS /
45 G UNSALTED
BUTTER

⅓ CUP / 80 ML
WHITE WINE

½ CUP / 120 ML
VEAL STOCK

This is a famous Roman dish, found in most trattorias in the capital. It's named *saltimbocca* because it is so good that it "jumps in the mouth." Making this delicious veal brings back memories of rented houses all over Italy, of summers going to the market and finally getting the proper thin "Italian cuts" of veal that French butchers are so reluctant to give you. Over the years, when we've wanted to re-create our Italian vacations, we always include saltimbocca and potatoes drenched in wine-infused gravy. Good-quality veal and ham are a must for this dish, but equally important, and perhaps my favorite herb of all, is the sage, which has to be fresh and abundant. In France, we have whole bushes of sage in our vegetable garden, and in Torino, the first thing we planted in pots on our terrace were generous amounts of sage. I like to cut more than I need and to stick the rest in a vase in my kitchen—a feast for my eyes and my nose.

1   Cover the cutlets with a sheet of plastic wrap and pound each with a meat pounder until ¼ inch / 6 mm thick. Season with salt and pepper.

2   Dust both sides of the veal as lightly as possible with cornstarch. Place a slice of prosciutto on top of each cutlet and a sage leaf on top of that. Fasten the layers with a wooden toothpick.

3   In a large sauté pan, heat 2 tablespoons of the olive oil over high heat until very hot. Working in batches, add the veal cutlets, prosciutto side up. When the cutlets are lightly browned, 1 to 2 minutes, flip onto the other side and cook for just 3 seconds. Transfer to a large serving plate.

4   Reduce the heat to medium and add the remaining sage leaves to the pan. Add 2 tablespoons of the butter and heat until slightly sizzling. Add the wine and reduce for 2 minutes. Add the veal stock and reduce for 2 more minutes. Add the remaining 1 tablespoon butter and whisk to emulsify the sauce until thickened.

5   Immediately pour the sauce all over the veal cutlets and serve.

# ROAST PORK
## WITH BALSAMIC VINEGAR AND RED WINE

This is a recipe I've been cooking for years, inspired by rustic meals I've had in the Italian countryside. It's such an easy dish to make— you start with good-quality pork of course, and the olive oil and balsamic lend it a very tasty Italian flair. The inclusion of bay leaves is simply because we always have so much of it in our garden that I can't help but reach for it, if only to decorate the pan. I like to serve this dish with mashed potatoes or polenta to soak up all the heavenly sauce.

1   Preheat the oven to 350°F / 180°C.

2   Score the skinned side of the pork loin and season with salt and pepper. Sprinkle the thyme and fennel seeds on both sides.

3   In a large skillet (or flameproof roasting pan), heat the olive oil over high heat. Add the pork loin skin side down and cook until the skin is golden. Turn on the other side and cook until golden brown, a couple of minutes longer. Pour in the balsamic vinegar, add the bay leaves, and turn the pork loin to coat. Let bubble and reduce for 2 minutes, then transfer to a roasting pan (if using the skillet) along with all the juices. Place the garlic cloves around the meat.

4   Transfer the roasting pan to the oven and roast until the meat is cooked through, about 1 hour 10 minutes. If you have a meat thermometer, it should read 145°F / 63°C at the thickest part of the roast. Halfway though, pour in the red wine. Check the oven regularly and add a bit of water if needed to prevent burning.

5   Let the meat rest for 10 good minutes before carving. Strain the pan sauce and drizzle it all over the meat once carved. Serve with mashed potatoes or polenta.

NOTE: *If possible, ask your butcher for the pork roast with the skin still attached.*

*Serves 6*

4½ POUNDS / 2 KG BONELESS PORK LOIN ROAST, WITH A GENEROUS LAYER OF FAT, TIED WITH STRING (SEE NOTE)

FINE SEA SALT AND FRESHLY GROUND BLACK PEPPER

A FEW SPRIGS OF FRESH THYME, LEAVES PICKED

1 TABLESPOON FENNEL SEEDS, CRUSHED WITH A MORTAR AND PESTLE

¼ CUP / 60 ML EXTRA-VIRGIN OLIVE OIL

1 CUP / 240 ML BALSAMIC VINEGAR

2 BAY LEAVES

15 GARLIC CLOVES, UNPEELED AND SMASHED

½ CUP / 120 ML RED WINE

MASHED POTATOES OR POLENTA, FOR SERVING

SECONDI

# MAIALE AL LATTE

*Pork Loin Stewed in Milk and Sage*

*Serves 4*

3 POUNDS / 1.4 KG
BONELESS PORK OR
VEAL LOIN, TIED
INTO A ROAST
(ASK YOUR BUTCHER
TO DO THIS)

FINE SEA SALT AND
FRESHLY GROUND
BLACK PEPPER

½ CUP / 120 ML
EXTRA-VIRGIN
OLIVE OIL

2 GARLIC CLOVES,
UNPEELED AND
SMASHED

10 FRESH SAGE
LEAVES

2 BAY LEAVES

1 SPRIG OF FRESH
ROSEMARY

1½ CUPS / 360 ML
WHOLE MILK

I have a weakness for all things cooked in milk. It's always fascinated me, the idea of something delicious drenched in milk, like taking a bath in milk and honey. It somehow makes every dish milder, more feminine, less aggressive. No herb goes better with meat and milk than sage; I often used that combination to cook farm chicken back in our house in France. So when I unearthed this old Venetian recipe, I knew I had to try it, and once I did, I knew it had to be in the book.

1   Generously season the roast with salt and pepper.

2   In a large, heavy saucepan, heat the olive oil over medium-high heat. Add the roast and garlic and brown the meat on all sides. Set the roast and garlic aside on a plate.

3   Add the sage, bay leaves, and rosemary to the oil in the pan and sauté for 1 minute. Return the roast to the pan and pour in the milk. Bring the milk to a simmer, then reduce the heat to low and cook, uncovered, turning the roast a few times, until the milk has reduced to a thick sauce and the meat is cooked through, at least 1 hour. If you have a meat thermometer, it should read 145°F / 63°C at the thickest part of the roast.

4   Remove the roast, cover with foil to keep warm, and let rest for at least 10 minutes.

5   Slice the roast and serve with the curdly milk sauce. (If you prefer a smoother sauce, simply strain the sauce through a fine-mesh sieve and blend it with an immersion blender.) Season with salt and pepper and serve.

# BRASATO AL BAROLO
## Beef Braised in Barolo Wine

6 WHOLE CLOVES

1 STAR ANISE

1 TABLESPOON BLACK
PEPPERCORNS

1 SMALL CINNAMON
STICK

1 SPRIG OF FRESH
ROSEMARY

1 SPRIG OF FRESH
THYME

1 BAY LEAF

3 TO 3½-POUND /
1.4 TO 1.6 KG
BONELESS BEEF ROAST

2 CELERY STALKS, CUT
INTO 1-INCH / 2.5 CM
CHUNKS

4 MEDIUM CARROTS,
PEELED AND CUT
INTO 1-INCH / 2.5 CM
ROUNDS

1 LARGE ONION,
COARSELY CHOPPED

1½ BOTTLES (750 ML
EACH) BAROLO WINE,
PLUS MORE IF NEEDED

FINE SEA SALT AND
FRESHLY GROUND
BLACK PEPPER

¼ CUP / 60 ML
EXTRA-VIRGIN
OLIVE OIL

1 TABLESPOON / 15 G
UNSALTED BUTTER

COOKED TAGLIATELLE
OR POLENTA, FOR
SERVING

**B**rasato is commonly found in most Piedmontese trattorias and res-taurants, but it's hardly a common dish. In fact, it's a dish fit for a king—a noble piece of meat braised for hours in fine wine. There is, however, risk involved. I've probably had more disappointments ordering this dish than any other, which is a shame because you start out with such wonderful ingredients that what follows should be easy. I can imagine the chefs of old cooking *brasato* for their masters, serving it with a shivering hand. A great *brasato* should be fork-tender, moist, and delicious. Too often the meat is dry and hard. A bad *brasato,* however, is not only inedible, but also involves wasting beef and a fine bottle of wine. This is not to say you shouldn't try this at home, but give it your best shot.

1   In a small piece of cheesecloth, place the cloves, star anise, peppercorns, and cinnamon stick. Tie closed with kitchen twine. Gather the rosemary, thyme, and bay leaf in a small bunch and tie together with kitchen twine to make a bouquet garni.

2   In a large bowl, combine the spice bag, bouquet garni, beef, celery, carrots, and onion. Pour in enough wine to cover everything. Cover with plastic wrap and refrigerate for 8 hours.

3   Remove the beef from the mixture and pat dry with paper towels. Reserve the marinade and vegetables.

4   Generously season all sides of the beef with salt and pepper. In a large Dutch oven, heat the olive oil and butter together over medium-high heat. Add the beef and brown on all sides until a nice crust forms all over, about 8 minutes. Remove from the pan and set aside.

5   Use a slotted spoon to transfer the vegetables from the marinade to the pot. Cook until softened, about 10 minutes. Return the meat to the pot. Season with salt and pepper. Remove the pan from the heat and add enough of the marinade until the liquid comes halfway up the beef.

6   Bring the wine to a boil over high heat. As soon as the wine begins
    to bubble, reduce the heat to low or medium-low to gently simmer.
    Cover and cook until the beef is very tender, 2 to 3 hours. After 1 hour,
    flip the meat onto the other side. After the second hour, turn it again
    so it gets all the right flavors everywhere. By then, the wine will have
    thickened and reduced by half.

7   Transfer the roast to a platter and cover with foil to rest for 10 minutes.

8   Bring the wine and vegetables back to a boil and reduce to a thick
    consistency, about 8 minutes. Season to taste. Slice the beef and
    spoon the sauce generously all over. Serve with tagliatelle or polenta.
    Generously spoon more of the sauce over each serving.

# *TAGLIATA*
## *WITH RADICCHIO*

*Serves 4*

4 TABLESPOONS
EXTRA-VIRGIN OLIVE
OIL

1 POUND / 450 G
BONELESS SIRLOIN
STEAK (AT LEAST
1 INCH / 2.5 CM
THICK)

FINE SEA SALT

3 GARLIC CLOVES,
UNPEELED AND
SMASHED

4 TO 6 SPRIGS OF
FRESH ROSEMARY

2 HEADS RADICCHIO,
CHOPPED

FRESHLY GROUND
BLACK PEPPER

 hroughout the year, this is the *secondi* we cook the most at home. We are blessed with incredible butchers on every corner in Torino, and Piedmontese culinary traditions are steeped in cooking with veal and beef. The quality is undeniable, and now that I've narrowed my butchers down to three, I know that I'll always get exactly what I want, as each has his personal best. After a satisfying plate of pasta or rice, there is nothing better than one or two strips of the finest meat, topped with a dash of garlic-infused olive oil perfumed with rosemary. At the bottom of the pan is the radicchio, which in all its bittersweet glory has one simple job: to soak up the juices.

1   Heat a heavy skillet over high heat. Add 2 tablespoons of the olive oil and heat until it is smoking hot. Season the steak with a little salt on each side and place in the pan for 25 seconds. Turn the steak over and fry for 25 seconds more. Repeat this process, turning the steak until crusty golden brown, a total of 2½ minutes. Remove the pan from the heat and transfer the steak to a wire rack set over a plate to catch the juices.

2   Let the pan cool for 1 minute. Add the garlic and rosemary sprigs to infuse the oil for 5 minutes. Add all the juices from the resting meat. Transfer the sauce to a small bowl.

3   Add the remaining 2 tablespoons olive oil to the pan and heat over medium heat. Add the chopped radicchio and cook, stirring frequently, until crisp-tender, about 3 minutes.

4   Place the radicchio in the center of a large serving plate. Thinly slice the steak and arrange on top of the radicchio. Season with salt and pepper. Drizzle with the reserved sauce, garnish with the rosemary, and serve.

# *CONTORNI*

side dish is by definition not the star of the show. It backs up the top billing, the steak, the roast, the meatballs. It quietly supports a good meal, making it more fulfilling than it would have been without. But a side dish is never really what it's all about.

However, it crossed my mind the other day that from the perspective of, say, spinach, which is mostly destined for a bit-part existence or a supporting role, the place to be is an Italian kitchen. No other kitchen gives so much weight to the character actors, the bitter greens and purples, the crunchy salads, the multicolored beans. A great restaurant in another country might offer a few standard fillers: the salad, the fries, the green beans. They are there because they need to be. But in Italy, the side show is interesting on its own. The everchanging, seasonal, and sometimes experimental little delights that you'll find even in the smallest, simplest trattorias. Not content to offer simply a mixed salad, they delight in reciting what's peaking at the moment. Maybe a bit of porcini? Some bitter greens? Some wild herbs from our vineyards? I've been known to order every side dish in a restaurant and nothing else. But only in Italy.

# INSALATA DI CARCIOFINI
## Artichoke Salad

*Serves 4 to 6*

12 BABY ARTICHOKES

SPARKLING WATER,
COLD

EXTRA-VIRGIN
OLIVE OIL

FINE SEA SALT

A FEW SQUEEZES OF
FRESH LEMON JUICE

A BLOCK OF
PARMESAN CHEESE

One of the delights of shopping for vegetables in Venice are the stunning baby artichokes from the nearby island of Sant'Erasmo. Long a kitchen garden for Venice itself, the island is home to a quiet agricultural community that produces many of the vegetables consumed in the city. These violet and slightly sweet artichokes are considered some of the finest in Italy, irresistible when on display at farmers' markets, laid out like bouquets of flowers. Our friends in Venice, the Romanellis, introduced us to this delicate and flavorful salad of raw, thinly sliced artichokes, topped with Parmesan, lemon, and olive oil.

1   Remove the outer layer of leaves from the artichokes, chop the spiky tip off, and trim the base. Slice as thinly as possible.

2   Place the sliced artichokes in a large bowl of cold sparkling water for 5 minutes. Drain the artichokes and pat dry gently.

3   In a large serving bowl, toss the artichokes with extra-virgin olive oil, season with salt, and add a few squeezes of lemon juice. Shave a few slices of Parmesan cheese on top and serve.

THIS IS MY FAVORITE STORY ABOUT ROME. A MAN AND A WOMAN FALL in love and decide to get married. The wedding is the smallest affair, but the most glamorous: a wedding lunch that lasts five hours, at the Grand Véfour, the most fabulous restaurant in Paris. Only six people in attendance. Krug Champagne, ravioli stuffed with foie gras, pigeon stuffed with foie gras, the finest Burgundy, desserts that never, ever end. Then a tipsy plane ride to Rome. A small, lovely hotel. It's too late for a proper meal, but that's fine. In fact, it's great. Sometimes pizza at midnight is the best food you'll ever have. Especially on your wedding night, after a lunch like that. Besides, wedding nights don't really finish at midnight, and a heavy dinner is never a good idea.

Rome is very special to me; it's an unreal place. I wrote that the people of Venice don't see the tourists anymore, that they treat them like ghosts or they're like ghosts themselves. In Rome, I'm like that. It's me and the city, and I'm the ghost. And Rome speaks to me. Right in the center, off via del Corso, is a museum that has my heart. Galleria Doria Pamphilj, the palazzo of a big family from a time gone by, with gorgeous art, imposing rooms, but also the family rooms on display, sometimes. They have a couple of Caravaggios, a masterpiece by Velázquez—the visit is worth it if only for those. But somehow, there is much more to it for me: I feel at home there and I always go twice. First alone, and then with those of my family who want to join. But I need that alone trip.

Like many cities of similar stature (or maybe there are none of those), Rome can never be visited once. The first visit is just a taste. An orientation. Trying to grasp the enormity of it all, even if the center is quite compact. How can it be, in such a small place, that there is so much. Of course, Rome is full of visitors, how could it not be. Largely, I don't mind it; to do so would be selfish. It is something you get used to. Like Venice, the crowds are all condensed in a very small area, and just outside that small circle, there is normal life. But I would love, just once, to get the private tour, after closing, when the streets are deserted. When the city would be all mine for a brief moment. To walk down the Spanish Steps and be the only one there, to stand in a deserted piazza del Popolo and admire it, have a perfect macchiato. (Wait, can I still do that if I'm the only person in Rome?)

Rome is where I finally fell in love with Italian food. I always really liked it, who doesn't, but French and Chinese food had my heart. Rome is where I saw the whole picture, eating like a Roman, embracing traditions. You can love Italian food, go to Italian restaurants all the time, but never really eat like an Italian. Rome is where I first did that. We went back every year, on our anniversary, for a few years. We've brought the kids, all eight of them. More than once. We've tried a few new things, we've explored the surrounding countryside, the coast. But our Roman trips are very repetitive, imitating our honeymoon—as if we don't want the city to be anything else. When we're in Rome, we want to feel like it. It's not that we don't care about some great new place that opened. Yes, we want to go there, but we want to go to our places more, and we never have time to do anything else. Sunday lunch at Piperno, drinks at the Locarno, cacio e pepe and pizza bianca at Roscioli. It's the *Groundhog Day* of our dreams, a self-inflicted exile from anything new. Rome is our city.

# PUNTARELLE ALLA ROMANA

Puntarelle is a wonderful vegetable that's only available in the colder months. Adding the "alla Romana" means adding anchovies, oil, and a hint of garlic. It's crunchy and delicious and a great way to start a meal. Oddur loves this dish more than any other salad and often chooses his restaurants based on whether they have it or not. Puntarelle is also the source of many of our arguments. Well, not the puntarelle, but the garlic. He always puts in too much, as if he were still in France. Italians are more careful with garlic. A hint is enough. And this is a hint to my husband.

1   In a small bowl, combine the anchovies with the garlic, olive oil, and vinegar and whisk with a fork.

2   Remove and discard the outer leaves of the puntarelle. Detach the hollow stalks and cut each in half lengthwise, then lengthwise again into strips ¼ inch / 6 mm wide. Fill a large bowl with ice cubes and cold water and place the puntarelle strips in the bowl of ice water for 30 minutes.

3   Drain the puntarelle and gently pat dry with paper towels. Discard the garlic from the dressing. In a large serving bowl, toss the puntarelle with the dressing. Season lightly with salt and pepper (the anchovies are already quite salty). Serve immediately.

*Serves 4*

3 OIL-PACKED
ANCHOVY FILLETS,
FINELY CHOPPED

2 GARLIC CLOVES,
SMASHED AND
PEELED

3 TABLESPOONS
EXTRA-VIRGIN
OLIVE OIL

1 TABLESPOON RED
WINE VINEGAR

1 HEAD (1 POUND /
450 G) PUNTARELLE

FINE SEA SALT AND
FRESHLY GROUND
BLACK PEPPER

# CHICORY
## WITH GARLIC AND PEPERONCINI

*Serves 4*

2¼ POUNDS /
1 KG CHICORY OR
DANDELION GREENS,
LEAVES SEPARATED

4 TABLESPOONS
EXTRA-VIRGIN
OLIVE OIL

1 GARLIC CLOVE,
SMASHED AND
PEELED

½ TEASPOON FINE
SEA SALT

PINCH OF FRESH OR
DRIED CHILE PEPPERS

A lovely alternative to serving spinach with meat or fish is this simple dish I first had in Rome many years ago. This bitter vegetable can be cooked exactly like spinach with oil and garlic, and I like adding a bit of chile to counter the bitterness. You can serve this side dish whenever you would otherwise have spinach, but want more bite.

1   Bring a large pot of water to a boil.

2   Add the chicory and cook until tender, about 10 minutes. Drain well, squeezing out as much water as possible.

3   In a medium sauté pan, heat the olive oil and garlic over medium heat. Add the chicory, salt, and pepper flakes. Cook, tossing gently, for 10 minutes, until further softened and coated with oil. Serve immediately.

THE LARGEST OF ITALY'S TWENTY REGIONS, DETACHED BY SEA, WITH a grand history all its own and more rulers and a more diverse past than any part of the mainland—Sicily is very much a different Italy. The locals are Italians but also Sicilians, maybe more so. The region has more autonomy than most and more well-known associations. It also has more oranges. If Abruzzo was used as a kitchen garden for Milano, then Sicily is a king's garden. The produce here is unrivaled, in quality and in volume. Sometimes it seems Sicily produces most of what's eaten in Italy. And the produce is well respected, too. In markets all over the country, it's a sign of prestige if the tomatoes come from Sicily, or if the oranges were grown there. It is a common sight to see a merchant at a market with two stacks of something—almonds, clementines, lemons, tomatoes—with one bunch more costly than the other: the one from Sicily.

It's an island of endless allure and endless drama. Pick your favorite Sicily: *The Godfather* or *Il Gattopardo*. An island with one of the most beautiful active volcanoes in the world, Mount Etna. The surrounding soil produces wonderful wines, which are rising, as are other Sicilian wines. To me, Sicily is distinctly Italian, but one step further in the third dimension. A little more unruly and free, higher in spirit if not in function. More iconic than anything, but you can't put your finger on it. That ineffable quality is there in the beauty of Taormina, as good as Amalfi but with cactuses and, perhaps, more mystery. The rough charm of Catania and Palermo, towns with endless promise of intrigue and danger. That guy asking for your number who's an actual Mafioso, or maybe just a common scoundrel. Or are they the same thing?

The food is to die for. Of course. One of my favorite things in the world is an almond granita. In Sicily, they have the best, and in Noto, at Caffè Sicilia, they have maybe the best in the world. As a friend said, "We can discuss the cannoli, but the almond granita there is the very best in the world." So we drove to Noto to find out, but they were closed. That day and that week. I was devastated, ruined. I refused to get out of the car. So we didn't and kept driving to have lunch in Ortigia instead, which was lovely. All over Sicily, they have great food. Let's start with dessert. Cannoli. I always loved the idea of a good one. It may be my favorite Italian dessert. Cassata, so dreamy, so iconic and maybe the most beautiful cake. And the crispelle. Then the eggplant trio: *pasta alla norma,* caponata, parmigiana (Neapolitan? Sicilian? Never mind, they used to be the same kingdom). Everybody's favorite snack, the deep-fried and delicious arancini rice balls and the *panelle,* chickpea fritters. The roast lamb or suckling pig.

Sicily is so many things at the same time. Mostly, it's a very beautiful place. We all know the *Godfather* connotation, glorified—wrongly probably, but still a classic. My favorite image of Sicily is from *Il Gattopardo* (which means "the leopard"), one of Italy's best loved and most popular pieces of historical fiction. The titular character was an endlessly elegant aristocrat at the time of the Risorgimento, the unification. Powerless to withstand the red shirts of Garibaldi, he mourned the end of the old, respectable, glorious ways. I can see him in his dressing gown, on the terrace of his palazzo, overlooking the orange groves, the almond plantation. Some of that world remains, some is gone. But a new world has emerged, youthful and energetic, with its own style, preserving the old ways with respect and humility.

Our good Italians in Sicily are quite the couple: Fiona and Diego. She's a Florentine like her twin sister, Nencia, in Umbria. A tale of two princesses. He is the son of Giuseppe San Giuliano, the last leopard, for real. But really, just two of the most enchanting people: a fairy and a charmer (who, to my daughter's delight, can move his ears in any direction). They hosted us at their magical estate in San Giuliano and life will never be the same. Imagine waking up with endless acres of orange trees as your morning view. Mystical gardens. Wild dogs. Fig trees and a private cemetery where death doesn't seem so final. When I asked Fiona to contribute to this book, lend me some fairy dust, she mulled it over a bit: She was thinking citrus, but in the end we must share her devil's sauce (page 256), which matches her sister's contribution (page 45) to a tee.

# FIONA'S DIAVOLA SAUCE

*Makes 1 small jar
(perfect for your
handbag)*

1 HABANERO PEPPER

½ MEDIUM YELLOW
ONION

DRIZZLE OF
EXTRA-VIRGIN
OLIVE OIL

PINCH OF FINE
SEA SALT

iona Corsini is a woman out of a fairy tale, or even a fairy her-self. She's kind, big-hearted, and talented, a wonderful artist who paints the most beautiful watercolors, often of her gardens in Sicily. She adores good food, is in love with citrus, and always has flowers in her hair. We stayed with her and her husband at their property, the magical San Giuliano, in Sicily, not far from Siracusa. Being among the citrus fields, palm trees, and secret gardens was a delight, and I noticed she always had this little bottle with her whenever she sat down to eat. It's her little secret, a spicy sauce that can be used on anything, from breakfast to dinner, on eggs, in soups or pastas. Of course, I asked for the recipe, and here it is. The intriguing thing is that her twin, Nencia, also shared a recipe for the book, also with peppers (page 45)—one person, two bodies.

Combine all the ingredients together in a mini food processor (or in a jar with an immersion blender) and process until you get a smooth paste. Spoon the mixture into a small jar and serve. It keeps for about 1 week in the refrigerator.

# DESSERTS

# *DOLCI*

efore desserts, there might be cheese, but in my case, rarely. I adore Italian cheeses; Gorgonzola is one of my all-time delights. But I'd rather have him on his own with a glass or a bottle of red. At this time of the meal, I'm usually ready to go sweet or go home. I love gelato, but hardly ever at the end of a meal—it's more of an afternoon delight, on vacation. (Or not on vacation.) Understated is how I'd describe Italian desserts. Some flour, some milk or cheese, not too sweet. A truly great panna cotta. A cake made from ricotta and pine nuts. Hazelnuts. Chocolate. Biscotti and sweet wine, holy wine. Only half sweet and half not; dolce is a balanced affair. A sponge cake on the side, with chilled, fresh seasonal fruit. After a meal like the ones you have in Italy, I'd be happy with a pear. Served on a plate, a white napkin on the side, silver cutlery. A pear tastes different when you cut it with silver. Apricots and cherries in a bucket of ice water, just fresh. Ricotta with honey or chocolate. If Italian cooking is ingredient-based, this is where it really happens. All good Italian desserts have one thing in common: They are not too much, but just right.

# PASTIERA CAKE

## PASTRY

1½ CUPS / 300 G
ALL-PURPOSE FLOUR

9 TABLESPOONS /
130 G UNSALTED
BUTTER, PLUS MORE
FOR THE PAN

PINCH OF FINE SEA
SALT

3 LARGE EGG YOLKS

¾ CUP / 150 G
SUPERFINE SUGAR

## WHEAT CREAM

1⅔ CUPS / 400 ML
WHOLE MILK

2 CUPS /
300 G COOKED
WHEATBERRIES

2 TABLESPOONS /
30 G UNSALTED
BUTTER

GRATED ZEST
OF 1 LEMON

GRATED ZEST
OF 1 ORANGE

1 TEASPOON
SUPERFINE SUGAR

PINCH OF FINE
SEA SALT

PINCH OF GROUND
CINNAMON

he official cake of Napoli is the revered *pastiera*, originally made for Easter but now enjoyed year-round. It seems to be everywhere, in restaurants and family homes, sold in tins on street corners. Like so many Italian desserts, a *pastiera* is made with ricotta and eggs, and unlike many pastries that are best enjoyed fresh out of the oven, a *pastiera* is at its finest when you let it rest a few days. The wheat cream uses cooked wheatberries, a precooked grain called *grano cotto,* sold in jars or cans and used for baking. Alternatively, you can improvise, using cooked risotto. This version is from the lovely but fiery Carolina, pastry chef of Mimì alla Ferrovia in Napoli. Carolina is the fiancée of the owner's son, who also happens to be the chef, but she's her own boss and takes orders from no one, a true Neapolitan woman.

1  **Make the pastry:** In a large bowl, mix the flour with the butter and salt with your fingers until you obtain a crumbly mixture. Mix in the egg yolks one at a time. Mix in the sugar. If necessary, add a few drops of cold water to obtain a homogeneous mixture. Form the dough into a ball and wrap in plastic wrap. Let rest for at least 2 hours in the refrigerator.

2  **Make the wheat cream:** In a large saucepan, heat the milk over low heat. When it comes to a simmer, add the wheat, butter, lemon zest, orange zest, sugar, salt, and cinnamon. Stir constantly and, when the mixture becomes creamy, about 10 minutes, remove from the heat. Transfer to a large bowl and cover with plastic wrap. Let cool completely at room temperature.

3  Preheat the oven to 350°F / 180°C.

4  **Make the filling:** In a large bowl, combine the ricotta with the sugar and mix gently. Mix in the 6 egg yolks one at a time. Add the vanilla, cinnamon, orange zest, lemon zest, and the cooled wheat cream and mix gently. Fold in the candied fruits and orange flower extract.

5  In a separate large bowl, whisk the 6 egg whites until stiff peaks form. Gently fold into the filling mixture.

6   Generously grease a 10-inch / 25 cm springform pan with butter. On a lightly floured work surface, roll out the pastry to a thickness of about ⅛ inch/ 4 mm and line the prepared pan. Cut off the overhang and knead these dough scraps together. Roll out the pastry again and cut into long strips ½ inch / 1.25 cm wide. Pour the filling in the pastry-lined pan. Use the strips to make a lattice crisscrossed on top of the cake. Press the ends of the strips to adhere to the edges.

7   Transfer to the oven and bake for 20 minutes. Reduce the oven temperature to 320°F / 160°C and continue baking until golden brown, about another 50 minutes.

8   Let cool completely, then leave out overnight to set. Unmold and serve. Store in a cool, dry place for up to 6 days. (According to tradition, the *pastiera* should be baked on Maundy Thursday in order that it be very set by Easter Sunday.)

*FILLING*

17 OUNCES / 500 G SHEEP'S MILK RICOTTA CHEESE

1¾ CUPS / 350 G SUPERFINE SUGAR

6 LARGE EGGS, SEPARATED

1 TEASPOON VANILLA EXTRACT

PINCH OF GROUND CINNAMON

GRATED ZEST OF ½ ORANGE

GRATED ZEST OF ½ LEMON

1¾ CUPS / 250 G MIXED CANDIED FRUIT, CUT INTO SMALL CUBES

1 TEASPOON ORANGE FLOWER EXTRACT

# CACHI AL RUM
## Persimmons with Vanilla and Rum

*Serves 4*

½ cup / 120 ml rum

1 vanilla bean,
split lengthwise

4 ripe persimmons,
chilled before
serving

ometimes a little fruit is all you need, especially after a heavy meal. In summer, a bowl of cherries and apricots might do the trick, but in winter, I love to have persimmons whenever I can, and they may even be my favorite fruit of all. The window to enjoy them is not very long, as they usually appear in late autumn and are gone before Christmas.

In Italy, they are often sold very ripe, which I like, and while having them on their own is ample joy, sprinkling them with a little vanilla-infused rum is even better.

1   Pour the rum into a small bowl. Scrape the vanilla seeds in and add the pod. Refrigerate and let the mixture infuse for at least 1 hour and up to 24 hours.

2   Just before serving, simply cut off the leaf-like calyx of the persimmons, then cut into quarters to open up the fruit like a flower. Scoop out the seeds and inner core if present. Transfer the fruit to a serving platter. Drizzle the vanilla-infused rum over the top and serve immediately.

# VANILLA CHESTNUT CREAM MADELEINES

I'm going out on a limb with the inclusion of this recipe. Madeleines are of course French. But in my defense, Torino as we know it was established by French dukes, and that influence is everywhere, not least in the kitchen. Everyone loves madeleines, one of my favorite recipes. Some desserts that I consider French have been appropriated by Italy and are very popular, like crème caramel and baba au rhum. So why not madeleines? Adding chestnuts gives them an Italian feel.

1   Preheat the oven to 400°F / 200°C. Butter two 12-cup madeleine pans.

2   In a large bowl, mix the eggs and granulated sugar. Stir in the flour and baking powder. In a medium bowl, combine the melted butter, rum, vanilla, and chestnut puree. Add the butter/chestnut mixture to the batter and mix with a wooden spoon until combined. Divide the batter among the madeleine molds.

3   Bake for 5 minutes, then reduce the oven temperature to 350°F / 180°C. Continue baking until golden brown, another 8 minutes. Unmold immediately and let cool on a wire rack for 1 minute before serving. Dust lightly with powdered sugar.

*Makes 20 to 24 madeleines*

2 LARGE EGGS

½ CUP / 100 G GRANULATED SUGAR

¾ CUP PLUS 2 TABLESPOONS / 100 G ALL-PURPOSE FLOUR

1 TEASPOON BAKING POWDER

6 TABLESPOONS / 90 G UNSALTED BUTTER, MELTED, PLUS MORE FOR THE PANS

2 TABLESPOONS RUM

1 TEASPOON VANILLA EXTRACT

7 OUNCES / 200 G SWEETENED CHESTNUT PUREE

POWDERED SUGAR, FOR DUSTING

# TORTA TENERINA
## Traditional Chocolate Cake

*Serves 8*

14 TABLESPOONS /
200 G UNSALTED
BUTTER, AT ROOM
TEMPERATURE,
PLUS MORE FOR
GREASING THE PAN

14 OUNCES / 400 G
DARK CHOCOLATE
(70% CACAO),
COARSELY CHOPPED

5 LARGE EGGS,
SEPARATED

¾ CUP / 150 G
SUPERFINE SUGAR

½ TEASPOON FINE
SEA SALT

6 TABLESPOONS /
45 G ALL-PURPOSE
FLOUR, SIFTED

FRESH BERRIES, FOR
GARNISH (OPTIONAL)

POWDERED SUGAR,
FOR DUSTING

The cuisine of Emilia-Romagna is both one of my favorites and the most celebrated in all of Italy. Just think about mortadella, tortellini, lasagne, tagliatelle with ragù. After such a meal, one would think that a dessert would be out of the question. That's when they bring out the *tenerina*, a rich, moist, and delicious chocolate cake. And who am I to disagree?

1 Preheat the oven to 300°F / 150°C. Grease a 10-inch / 25 cm cake pan with butter and line the bottom with a round of parchment paper.

2 In a heatproof bowl set over a saucepan of simmering water, stir the chocolate until melted. Remove the bowl from the pan, stir in the butter, and let cool for 10 minutes.

3 In a medium bowl, whisk together the egg yolks and superfine sugar until light and fluffy, about 4 minutes. In a separate bowl, whisk the egg whites with the salt until stiff peaks form.

4 Stir the melted chocolate / butter mixture into the egg yolk mixture. Fold in the flour until combined. Gently fold in the beaten egg whites. Pour the batter into the prepared pan.

5 Transfer to the oven and bake until the top is firm to the touch, about 30 minutes. Let cool in the pan for at least 1 hour before unmolding.

6 Serve topped with berries, if desired, and a dusting of powdered sugar.

# ZABAIONE

*Z*abaione is a national treasure of Italy, and no fewer than three regions claim it as their invention. I won't get into that, but I'm giving it to Emilia-Romagna for practical reasons: Tuscany is not included in this book and Piemonte already has panna cotta. (By the way, Lombardia probably claims this dessert as well.) The origins of this particular recipe, however, are not in dispute. I got it from the place where I have enjoyed *zabaione* the most, Antica Trattoria della Pesa in Milano. In winter they make a hot, foamy, and delicious *zabaione*; just watching Pasquale, the chef at Antica, makes my head spin, so fast does he whisk the cream, and with such ease. In summer they serve my favorite, the same thing chilled, plus whipped cream. They let the *zabaione* cool down, then fold in the cream and chill, serving it more like a custard.

In a medium saucepan, combine the Marsala, white wine, egg yolks, sugar, and 4 teaspoons / 20 ml water. Whisk everything together over low heat for 30 seconds. Then, removing the pan from the heat every 10 seconds, continue to whisk constantly until the custard starts to thicken and coat the back of a spoon, 10 to 12 minutes total. Serve immediately.

*Serves 4*

¼ CUP / 60 ML DRY
MARSALA WINE

¼ CUP / 60 ML DRY
WHITE WINE

8 LARGE EGG YOLKS

1 CUP / 200 G SUGAR

## CHILLED ZABAIONE
### *My favorite, perfect for summer months*

Make the *zabaione* as directed and let cool completely. Cover with plastic wrap and refrigerate for at least 2 hours to chill. In a large bowl, whip 1½ cups / 350 ml cold heavy cream until thick and stiff and fold into the cold *zabaione*. Serve immediately.

# CASSATELLE
*Ricotta Cream Fritters*

*Makes 18 fritters*

7 TABLESPOONS
WHITE WINE

3 TABLESPOONS
EXTRA-VIRGIN
OLIVE OIL

2 CUPS / 240 G
SEMOLINA FLOUR

PINCH OF FINE SEA
SALT

1 CUP / 250 G
WHOLE-MILK
RICOTTA CHEESE
(PREFERABLY
SHEEP'S MILK)

3 TABLESPOONS
GRANULATED SUGAR

½ TEASPOON
GROUND CINNAMON,
PLUS MORE FOR
DUSTING

ALL-PURPOSE FLOUR,
FOR DUSTING

EXTRA-VIRGIN OLIVE
OR VEGETABLE OIL,
FOR DEEP-FRYING

POWDERED SUGAR,
FOR DUSTING

hen I visited Fabrizia Lanza at her cooking school in Sicily last November, she happened to be making these wonderful deep-fried, ricotta-filled half-moons. We were meant to have lunch together, and as I entered Fabrizia's kitchen, I saw these beautiful, delicious-looking fritters. I wasn't sure she'd serve them for lunch, but fortunately she did—and oh my! I immediately asked her to share the recipe, which she was pleased to do, then Oddur shot them quickly in her kitchen window. On another day, we would have missed them. Lucky moons!

1   In a small saucepan, heat the wine and olive oil together until warm (not hot) over medium-low heat.

2   On a work surface, pile up the semolina flour and make a well in the center. Add the warm wine / oil mixture and the salt, then carefully work it in and knead together until a dough forms.

3   In a medium bowl, stir together the ricotta, granulated sugar, and cinnamon and set the filling aside.

4   Divide the dough into 4 portions. Working with one portion at a time, flatten with a rolling pin. Set a pasta machine to its thickest setting. Roll the dough through the machine about five times at this setting, folding the dough in half before re-rolling it. When it is very even, switch the pasta machine to the next thinnest setting and roll it through two or three times more, folding it before re-rolling. Move the dial to the next setting and roll it through two or three more times, repeating the process until you get to the thinnest setting possible.

5   On a floured work surface, lay out the sheet of dough and cut out rounds with a 4-inch / 10 cm cookie cutter. On each round of dough, place a spoonful of ricotta filling just off center. Moisten the edges of the dough, fold over, and pinch to seal. Repeat with the remaining dough and filling.

6  Pour 1¼ inches / 3 cm oil into a large, high-sided pan. Heat the oil over medium-high heat. To test if the oil is ready, drop a 1-inch square of bread into the oil. If it takes 60 seconds to brown, then the oil is ready. Working in batches, deep-fry the half-moons, flipping occasionally, until deeply golden, about 3 minutes. Drain on paper towels, then dust with powdered sugar and cinnamon. Serve warm.

# VANILLA RICOTTA CREAM
## WITH CHOCOLATE SAUCE
## AND ORANGE ZEST

*Serves 4*

16 OUNCES / 450 G
WHOLE-MILK
RICOTTA CHEESE

1 CUP / 250 ML
HEAVY CREAM

1 VANILLA BEAN,
SPLIT LENGTHWISE

5 OUNCES / 150 G
DARK CHOCOLATE
(70% CACAO)

GRATED ZEST OF
1 ORANGE

 This is the dessert I make when I have little or no time but still want to offer my guests some homemade (or shall we say prepared) sweets at the end of the meal. Inspired by a dish we had in Umbria some years ago, I was struck by the sheer brilliance of this extremely simple but satisfying dessert. It's not too sweet either, and the orange zest goes so well with the chocolate.

1   Drain the ricotta in a fine-mesh sieve for 10 minutes. In a large bowl, combine the drained ricotta and cream. Scrape in the vanilla seeds and whisk until thick and creamy with soft peaks. Refrigerate for about 15 minutes.

2   Meanwhile, in a heatproof bowl set over a saucepan of simmering water, stir the chocolate until melted. Remove from the heat.

3   On serving plates, place a little nest of ricotta cream. Drizzle with the melted chocolate, sprinkle with the orange zest, and serve.

# TORTA DELLA NONNA
## *Grandma's Cake*

*Serves 8*

### PASTRY

1⅔ CUPS / 200 G
ALL-PURPOSE FLOUR,
PLUS MORE FOR
DUSTING

¼ CUP / 30 G
CORNSTARCH

⅓ CUP / 65 G
GRANULATED SUGAR

1 TEASPOON VANILLA
EXTRACT

FINELY GRATED ZEST
OF ½ LEMON

PINCH OF FINE SEA
SALT

8 TABLESPOONS /
120 G COLD UNSALTED
BUTTER, CUT INTO
SMALL CUBES

2 LARGE EGG YOLKS

2 TABLESPOONS
ICE-COLD WATER

### FILLING

1¼ CUPS / 300 ML
WHOLE MILK

¾ CUP PLUS
1 TABLESPOON /
200 ML HEAVY CREAM

GRATED ZEST
OF 1 LEMON

One of our favorite desserts is this ultraclassic, pine nut–covered, custard-filled cake that has captured my imagination for as long as I've been going to Italy. I used to think you could find it on most restaurant menus in the country, but strangely enough that's not the case—which is why I always order it when I get the chance. Unfortunately, a *torta della nonna* just means "grandma's cake," so I might be served something that I'm not expecting, but this *torta* here is the real thing.

1  Preheat the oven to 375°F / 190°C.

2  **Make the pastry:** In a large bowl, combine the flour, cornstarch, granulated sugar, vanilla, lemon zest, and salt. Add the butter and work into the flour with the tips of your fingers until it breaks down into fine crumbs. Add the egg yolks and ice-cold water and mix until the dough is smooth and homogeneous. Wrap the dough in plastic wrap and let rest in the fridge for at least 30 minutes or up to 24 hours.

3  **Meanwhile, make the filling:** In a medium saucepan, combine the milk, cream, and lemon zest. Heat over medium-low heat until just warm. In a small bowl, mix the flour with the granulated sugar. Slowly stir the flour mixture into the milk and cream. Cook, stirring constantly, until it comes to a simmer, about 5 minutes. Transfer to a medium bowl and let cool for 15 minutes before covering with plastic wrap pressed to the surface. Refrigerate until chilled.

4  Divide the dough in half and form into disks. Place a disk of dough on a sheet of flour-dusted parchment paper. Roll out to ⅛ inch / 3 mm thick and transfer (still on the parchment) to a tray. Repeat with the second disk of dough. Place the tray in the refrigerator for 10 minutes to stiffen the dough slightly.

5  Line a 9-inch / 23 cm tart pan with one of the crusts and fill with the hopefully-not-warm-anymore cream. Place the second crust on top. Pinch the edges of the crusts together and roll them down to form a rim. Spread the pine nuts on top.

6  Transfer to the oven and bake until the crust is golden, 30 to 40 minutes. Let cool for at least 45 minutes, carefully unmold, then dust all over with powdered sugar before serving. The kids love it cold the next day because of how firm the creamy custard gets!

⅓ CUP / 40 G
ALL-PURPOSE FLOUR

¾ CUP / 150 G
GRANULATED SUGAR

½ CUP / 80 G
PINE NUTS

POWDERED SUGAR,
FOR DUSTING

# *TORTA ALLE MANDORLE*
## *Almond Cake*

**L**et's start with the fact that I love almonds. I can never resist an almond granita, or anything, really, that has almonds in it. Which is why, when I discussed with Ferigo Foscari which recipes from his family's cookbook we should borrow, my eyes wandered to this one. Rosanna, the resident cook, made it to perfection for us, but even more heartwarming was the way the Foscari family talked about their favorite cake. It was almost Proustian: Everybody's face lit up and they were taken back to another time. The power of a simple cake, in the most beautiful house in the world.

1   Preheat the oven to 350°F / 180°C. Line the bottom of a 9-inch / 23 cm cake pan with a round of parchment paper.

2   In a large bowl, stir together the almond flour and lemon zest. Whisk in the egg yolks one at a time, the superfine sugar, and the milk until smooth. In a separate medium bowl, whisk the egg whites until stiff peaks form. Gently fold the beaten whites into the batter. Pour the batter into the lined pan.

3   Transfer to the oven and bake until a skewer or cake tester inserted into the center comes out clean, about 40 minutes. Let the cake cool in the pan for 10 minutes, then unmold onto a serving plate. Dust with powdered sugar before serving.

*Serves 6*

2 CUPS / 250 G
ALMOND FLOUR

GRATED ZEST
OF 1 LEMON

5 LARGE EGGS,
SEPARATED

1¼ CUPS / 250 G
SUPERFINE SUGAR

1 CUP / 240 ML
WHOLE MILK

POWDERED SUGAR,
FOR DUSTING

# TORTA DI NOCCIOLE
## *Hazelnut Cake*

### *Serves 8*

⅓ CUP / 80 G
UNSALTED
BUTTER, AT ROOM
TEMPERATURE, PLUS
MORE FOR GREASING
THE PAN

ALL-PURPOSE FLOUR,
FOR DUSTING THE
PAN

2 CUPS / 300 G
BLANCHED
HAZELNUTS

¼ CUP / 30 G
CORNSTARCH

2 TEASPOONS BAKING
POWDER

PINCH OF FINE
SEA SALT

2 TABLESPOONS
UNSWEETENED
COCOA POWDER

1 CUP / 200 G SUGAR

¼ CUP / 60 G
HAZELNUT PASTE
(SEE NOTE)

3 LARGE EGGS

 iemonte is a land of gastronomic wealth. The legendary wines, the white truffles of Alba. Genius dishes like vitello tonnato. Panna cotta. Agnolotti. How can humble hazelnuts ever get any attention? The competition is frightening. The odds staggering. Will anyone ever notice them? They are, after all, just nuts. Right next to some of the best wines in the world grow, in my opinion, the very best hazelnuts in the world. The "Nocciole del Piemonte." They deserve no less attention than the white truffles. Every time I go back to France, my friends beg me to bring them bags of roasted hazelnuts. The nuts go with everything. They are healthy. I have them in the morning, between meals, in the evening. I love them without guilt or fear. And I love to use them in my cooking.

1   Preheat the oven to 350°F / 180°C. Grease a 9-inch / 23 cm cake pan with butter and dust with flour.

2   Put the hazelnuts on a baking sheet and roast until they are golden brown, about 10 minutes, giving the pan a shake halfway through. Set aside to cool.

3   Place two-thirds of the hazelnuts in a food processor and pulse until they are finely ground. Transfer to a large bowl. Pulse the remaining hazelnuts until coarsely ground, like the consistency of coarse sand. Add to the bowl of finely ground hazelnuts. Stir in the cornstarch, baking powder, salt, and cocoa powder.

4   In a medium bowl, combine the butter, sugar, and hazelnut paste. Whisk until smooth. Add the eggs and continue to whisk until creamy. Fold into the ground hazelnut mixture until smooth. Scrape the batter into the prepared cake pan.

5   Transfer to the oven and bake until a skewer inserted into the center comes out clean, about 30 minutes. Let cool in the pan for 10 minutes. Unmold and serve.

NOTE: *If you can't find hazelnut paste, substitute chocolate-hazelnut spread.*

# PANNA COTTA

Panna cotta is easily one of the best-known Italian desserts, one that has not only traveled Italy but the whole world. Piemonte, however, doesn't get much credit for this recipe outside of the region; in fact, I only realized it came from here a few years ago. Of course, it makes sense, the strong French cooking traditions (and all those cows).

Panna cotta literally means "cooked cream," which is of course what it is. Unlike custard, which uses egg yolks, gelatin is used to thicken panna cotta, but you shouldn't notice it—a true panna cotta feels rich and creamy, never gel-ified.

1   In a medium saucepan, combine the milk, cream, and sugar. Scrape in the vanilla seeds and add the pod, too. Stir over low heat until the sugar has dissolved, being careful not to let the milk boil, about 4 minutes. Remove from the heat. Add the softened gelatin and whisk until dissolved. Set aside and cool to room temperature.

2   Once cooled, remove the pod and give the mixture a good stir to evenly distribute the vanilla seeds. Divide the mixture among four 4-ounce / 125 ml ramekins (3½-inch/9 cm diameter, 1½-inches/4 cm deep). Transfer to the refrigerator and let set for at least 6 hours and up to 24 hours.

3   To serve, dip the bottom of the ramekins in a bowl of warm water for a few seconds to loosen. Flip and unmold onto a plate. If desired, serve with a fresh fruit coulis or chocolate or caramel sauce.

NOTE: *If you can't find gelatin sheets, use 2 teaspoons powdered gelatin, which should first be dissolved: Place 2 tablespoons boiling water in a small heatproof bowl. Sprinkle the gelatin powder over it and stir until the gelatin has dissolved. Stir into the milk mixture at the end of step 1, as directed.*

*Serves 4*

½ CUP / 120 ML WHOLE MILK

1⅔ CUPS / 400 ML HEAVY CREAM

⅓ CUP / 65 G SUGAR

1 VANILLA BEAN, SPLIT LENGTHWISE

2 GELATIN LEAVES (SEE NOTE), SOFTENED IN COLD WATER AND DRAINED

FRESH FRUIT COULIS, OR CHOCOLATE OR CARAMEL SAUCE, FOR SERVING (OPTIONAL)

# TORTA DI RICOTTA
## Ricotta Cheesecake

*Serves 8*

4 TABLESPOONS /
60 G UNSALTED
BUTTER, AT ROOM
TEMPERATURE, PLUS
MORE FOR GREASING
THE PAN

POWDERED SUGAR,
FOR DUSTING THE
PAN AND GARNISH

3 LARGE EGGS,
SEPARATED

1½ CUPS / 300 G
GRANULATED SUGAR

10 OUNCES / 300 G
WHOLE-MILK
ITALIAN-STYLE
RICOTTA CHEESE OR
DRAINED REGULAR
RICOTTA

2½ CUPS / 300 G
ALL-PURPOSE FLOUR

2 TEASPOONS BAKING
POWDER

½ CUP / 120 ML
WHOLE MILK

PINCH OF FINE
SEA SALT

As I've said before, I love the ritual of an Italian meal. After great antipasti, some nice tomato pasta, a great piece of meat, I still want dessert, but nothing too overpowering. Maybe something that goes well with a sip of sweet wine, a *passito* perhaps. That's when I'm in the mood for this Italian cheesecake. Not too heavy or overly sweet. Just a simple Italian cheesecake, gentle, subtle, and wonderful.

1   Preheat the oven to 350°F / 180°C. Grease a 10-inch / 25 cm springform pan with butter and dust with a little powdered sugar.

2   In a large bowl, combine the egg yolks, granulated sugar, and butter. Whisk until smooth, then add the ricotta and mix gently. Sift in the flour and baking powder and mix well. Stir in the milk.

3   In a separate large bowl, use a hand mixer with a whisk attachment or a whisk to beat the egg whites with a pinch of salt until stiff peaks form. Gently fold the beaten egg whites into the batter. Pour the batter into the prepared cake pan.

4   Transfer to the oven and bake until golden, 30 to 40 minutes. Let cool in the pan, then unmold the cake, dust with powdered sugar, and serve.

# CASTAGNOLE

*Sugar-Coated Fried Doughnuts*

These are delicious doughnut-like balls covered in sugar and traditionally served during *carnevale*. Sometimes when I throw dinner parties, I want to go over the top, and that's when I make several desserts, just because nobody needs them but everybody wants them. For such an occasion, I bring the *castagnole* out, stacked on a silver tray, served with Champagne.

*Makes about 30 pieces*

1 LARGE EGG

GRATED ZEST OF 1 LEMON

3 TABLESPOONS / 40 G UNSALTED BUTTER, AT ROOM TEMPERATURE

1 TABLESPOON ANISE LIQUEUR

1 VANILLA BEAN, SPLIT LENGTHWISE, OR 1 TEASPOON VANILLA EXTRACT

1⅔ CUPS / 200 G TIPO "00" FLOUR

1 TEASPOON BAKING POWDER

¼ CUP / 50 G SUPERFINE SUGAR, PLUS MORE FOR DREDGING

PINCH OF FINE SEA SALT

VEGETABLE OIL, FOR DEEP-FRYING

1 In a medium bowl, combine the egg, lemon zest, butter, and liqueur. Scrape in the vanilla seeds or add the vanilla extract and mix until smooth.

2 In a large bowl, mix the flour, baking powder, sugar, and salt and make a well in the center. Add the egg mixture to the well and, starting from the center, mix to combine with the flour. Knead the dough with your hands until it becomes a soft and supple, slightly sticky ball. Wrap it in plastic wrap and let rest for 10 minutes in the refrigerator.

3 Divide the dough into 3 portions. Roll each into a rope 1 inch / 2.5 cm in diameter. Cut crosswise into ⅓-inch / 1 cm pieces, then roll into perfect little balls using the palms of your hands.

4 Pour 2 inches / 5 cm oil into a large, high-sided pan. Heat the oil to about 325°F / 160°C over medium heat. You can test if the oil is hot enough by dropping in a small piece of dough. If the dough turns golden within seconds, the oil is ready.

5 Working in batches, fry the dough balls until golden and puffy, a few seconds or so on each side. Remove with a slotted spoon and drain on paper towels. Place some sugar in a shallow bowl and dredge the *castagnole* in it. Serve immediately.

# PISTACHIO AND LEMON POUND CAKE

W.e have such wonderful memories from our family vacations on the Amalfi Coast. Days of swimming in the sea, trips to Capri and Positano, pizzas close to midnight, feasts for lunch. We so enjoyed the walk down from Ravello to nearby Minori, loving that every inch of the trail was covered with lemon trees. This local cake, similar to the one the kids requested every day at teatime when they sat poolside, trembling in their towels, takes us back to those days.

1  Preheat the oven to 350°F / 180°C. Grease a 9 × 5-inch / 23 × 12 cm loaf pan with butter.

2  In a large bowl, beat the granulated sugar and butter with a whisk until creamy. Beat in the eggs one at a time. Add the yogurt and mix. Add the all-purpose flour, pistachio flour, two-thirds of the lemon zest, and the baking powder and gently mix. Stir in the pistachio paste. Pour the batter into the prepared pan.

3  Bake for 40 minutes, or until a long skewer or cake tester inserted into the center comes out clean. Let cool in the pan for 15 minutes, then unmold onto a rack.

4  Garnish with the chopped pistachios, remaining lemon zest, and a dusting of powdered sugar and serve.

NOTE: *If you can't find pistachio flour, process 3 ounces/90 g shelled unsalted pistachios in a food processor. If you also can't find pistachio paste, use 1½ cups/135 g pistachio flour (made from 5 ounces/140 g shelled pistachios).*

*Serves 6*

12 TABLESPOONS / 180 G UNSALTED BUTTER, AT ROOM TEMPERATURE, PLUS MORE FOR GREASING THE PAN

1 CUP / 200 G GRANULATED SUGAR

4 LARGE EGGS

½ CUP / 145 G WHOLE-MILK GREEK YOGURT

2 CUPS PLUS 2 TABLESPOONS / 250 G ALL-PURPOSE FLOUR, SIFTED

1 CUP / 90 G PISTACHIO FLOUR (SEE NOTE)

GRATED ZEST OF 1½ LEMONS

1 TABLESPOON BAKING POWDER

½ CUP / 60 G PISTACHIO PASTE (SEE NOTE)

2 TABLESPOONS FINELY CHOPPED UNSALTED PISTACHIOS

POWDERED SUGAR, FOR DUSTING

# PIZZELLE

*Makes about 28
triangles*

1¼ CUPS / 150 G
ALL-PURPOSE FLOUR

¾ TEASPOON BAKING
POWDER

PINCH OF FINE
SEA SALT

3 LARGE EGGS, AT
ROOM TEMPERATURE

½ CUP / 100 G SUGAR

4 TABLESPOONS /
60 ML UNSALTED
BUTTER, MELTED,
PLUS MORE FOR
BRUSHING THE
PIZZELLE IRON

1 TEASPOON VANILLA
EXTRACT

1 TEASPOON
ANISE EXTRACT
(OPTIONAL)

his is one of the sweets I most enjoy making. Maybe because I feel the antiquity of the recipe and its sense of history, as pizzelle are derived from ancient Roman recipes. The tool I use and recommend is the traditional iron that's held over a hot burner on the stove or over an open fire. The patterns are beautiful, and the crunchy, waffle-like cookies are delicious and ceremonial.

1   Preheat a pizzelle iron over medium heat. If you are using an electric pizzelle iron, switch it on according to the manufacturer's instructions.

2   In a medium bowl, sift together the flour, baking powder, and salt. Set aside.

3   In a large bowl, with an electric mixer fitted with the whisk attachment, beat the eggs until frothy. Add the sugar and continue to whisk until well blended and pale yellow. Add the melted butter, the vanilla extract, and anise extract (if using). Fold in the flour mixture until well combined.

4   Brush a little of the remaining melted butter onto the pizzelle iron. Drop 1 tablespoon of batter onto the hot iron, close the lid, and cook until slightly golden, 30 to 45 seconds, flipping halfway. Remove from the iron with the help of a fork. Transfer to a tray and let cool for 3 minutes before serving. Repeat with the remaining batter and more melted butter.

# PESCHE RIPIENE

*Stuffed Peaches with Amaretti Biscuits and Cocoa*

ome peach season, every restaurant and café in Piemonte offers this old-fashioned delight in various versions. It's such a granny dessert: Even in the fanciest restaurants it still feels homemade and heartwarming. My kids love to have this in the afternoon as a little teatime snack, and I'm always happy to make it. It's really just having fruit with a little sweet stuffing, and it's much more delicious and healthy than most things they'd otherwise want. It's also incredibly quick and easy to make.

1  Preheat the oven to 360°F / 180°C. Line a 9 × 13-inch / 23 × 33 cm baking pan or small roasting pan with parchment paper.

2  Cut a little slice off the curved lobe of each peach half so that they can sit flat in the pan, pitted side up. Reserve the pieces, chop finely, and set aside in a large bowl. Using a small spoon, scoop out a teaspoon of peach and place in the reserved bowl. (You will get a nicer cavity to place your filling.)

3  Add the amaretti or ladyfingers, cocoa powder, sugar, and egg yolk to the bowl of reserved peach pieces and crush everything coarsely with a fork.

4  Fill each peach half with the filling and place in the baking pan. Dot the top of the filling with the butter.

5  Bake until the peaches are golden and bubbling, 20 to 25 minutes. Serve warm or cold.

*Serves 4*

4 YELLOW PEACHES, HALVED AND PITTED

2 OUNCES / 60 G AMARETTI COOKIES, OR 5 LADYFINGERS

2 TABLESPOONS UNSWEETENED COCOA POWDER

1 TABLESPOON SUPERFINE SUGAR

1 EGG YOLK

2 TABLESPOONS / 30 G UNSALTED BUTTER

# LEMON MERINGUE CAKE

## Serves 8

### CAKE

UNSALTED BUTTER,
FOR GREASING
THE PANS

1⅔ CUPS / 200 G
ALL-PURPOSE FLOUR,
PLUS MORE FOR
DUSTING THE PANS

6 LARGE EGGS,
SEPARATED

1 CUP / 200 G
SUPERFINE SUGAR

1 TEASPOON VANILLA
EXTRACT

1 TEASPOON BAKING
POWDER

### LEMON CUSTARD

¾ CUP / 150 G
GRANULATED SUGAR

GRATED ZEST
OF 1 LEMON

JUICE OF 2 LEMONS

2 LARGE EGGS,
BEATEN

2 TABLESPOONS PLUS
2 TEASPOONS / 40 G
UNSALTED BUTTER

¾ CUP / 180 ML
HEAVY CREAM

These kind of cakes are often served in restaurants that consider themselves a little fancy, where the waiters have uniforms and the silverware is actually made of silver. Places with heavy tablecloths and high ceilings and wonderful desserts. One such place is Harry's Bar in Venice, a venerable institution that I wouldn't dream of visiting without ordering cake similar to this one. In other words, it's a fancy cake; it reminds me of '50s movies set in Italy, with pink, fluffy dresses . . . okay, I'm getting carried away here.

1 **Make the cake:** Preheat the oven to 350°F / 180°C. Butter and flour two 8-inch / 20 cm cake pans.

2 In a large bowl, beat the egg yolks with the superfine sugar and vanilla until light and fluffy. In a separate medium bowl, beat the egg whites until stiff peaks form. Very gently fold the beaten egg whites into the egg yolk mixture. Sift in the flour and baking powder and fold into the egg mixture to combine. Spoon the batter gently into the prepared cake pans.

3 Transfer to the oven and bake until golden and a skewer inserted into the center comes out clean, 15 to 20 minutes. Let cool in the pans on a wire rack for 5 minutes, then remove from the pans and set aside to cool completely. When cool, slice each cake horizontally with a long knife to make 4 layers total. Set aside.

4 **Make the lemon custard:** In a heatproof bowl set over a medium saucepan of simmering water, combine the granulated sugar, lemon zest, and lemon juice. Add the beaten eggs to the sugar/lemon mixture and cook over medium heat, stirring constantly, until the mixture is thickened, about 8 minutes. You can take the bowl off the heat while whisking to prevent overcooking. Remove from the heat and stir in the butter. Set aside to cool completely, then refrigerate for 2 hours until chilled through.

5  In a large bowl, whip the cream until stiff peaks form. Fold the whipped cream into the cooled lemon custard.

6  Line a cake platter with parchment paper and place a cake layer on top. Spread a generous layer of the lemon custard on the cake and add another cake layer on top. Repeat this procedure for each layer except the last one. Transfer to the refrigerator for at least 1 hour.

7  **Make the meringue topping:** In the metal bowl of a stand mixer set over a medium pot of simmering water, whisk together the superfine sugar, egg whites, vanilla, and lemon juice, whisking until the sugar is dissolved, about 3 minutes. Transfer the bowl to the mixer stand and fit the mixer with the whisk attachment. Beat on medium speed for 10 minutes. Increase the speed to high and beat until stiff, glossy peaks form, 10 to 15 minutes more.

8  With a spatula, spread the meringue mixture over the top of the cake to cover it entirely, forming decorative peaks by lifting the spatula as if you were forming waves. Spread a thin, even layer of meringue over the sides of the cake. Use a kitchen torch to brown the meringue on the top and on the sides. Chill for 30 minutes before serving.

*MERINGUE TOPPING*

1 CUP PLUS 2 TABLESPOONS / 220 G SUPERFINE SUGAR

4 LARGE EGG WHITES, AT ROOM TEMPERATURE

1 TEASPOON VANILLA EXTRACT

JUICE OF ½ LEMON

# *Epilogue*

How do you write the ending to a story that hasn't finished? And does this story even need an ending?

If it does, it ends in a kitchen—not mine but somebody else's. Perhaps in yours.

It ends with a pot on a stove, simmering water, and oil in a pan. It ends with a laid-out table, maybe some lit candles, and ideally, it ends with a lot of people sharing a meal. Hopefully, they'll love the meal. Most likely, they will. Even if you don't cook it perfectly or if the recipe isn't perfect (although I tried to make it so). They love each other and sharing a meal makes them love each other more.

Italian cooking is family cooking. Recipes born in family kitchens. Cooked by the families of those who grew the vegetables, raised or hunted the animals. Those who respected and valued the ingredients because they had intimate knowledge of how special they were, how much work went into making them. A great tomato, sliced open with a dash of freshly pressed olive oil—it's three ingredients. And one of them is love.

As for us, the Thorissons, who knows? Somehow I know that Italy will always be a part of our lives. Will we live here forever? Will we go back to France? I suspect that the answer lies somewhere in between.

It's about balance. That word is important to me, in every context. In relationships, in work, in cooking. Italian food has incredible balance. An Italian meal plays out like the finest music or work of fiction, with a beginning, middle, and end.

I hope you find the balance. I think I'm close.

# *Acknowledgments*

We often talk about the process of making something, discovering something, or even learning something about ourselves as being on an emotional and personal journey. Writing this book has been one of these journeys as well as an actual journey. One that took my family from France to Italy, where we met people, learned more about local food traditions, and found the best recipes and ingredients. The reception I have received—the kindness, generosity, openness, and wisdom of countless Italians—has left me humbled and grateful. It has also left me wiser on the subject of Italian food. I can never thank everyone enough. It goes without saying that this book would not have been possible without all of you. *Grazie* from the very bottom of my heart—you know who you are.

Of course this book could not have happened without my publishers, who are letting my dreams come true for the third book in a row. Your confidence in me, the quality of your team, and those who edit, design, produce, and market the book—you all are really like a dream cast in a movie about a woman writing an Italian cookbook. Thank you so much for everything.

And finally, very special thanks to my literary agent, Rica—here we go again.

# Index